WHERE TO GO IN THE BIBLE WHEN...

SCRIPTURE REFERENCE GUIDE

88 TOPICS

DR. DAVID JEREMIAH

DISCOVER THE

BIBLE'S ANSWERS

TO LIFE'S MOST

CHALLENGING

QUESTIONS.

Introduction

Checking the inventory of the two largest online booksellers in the "Self-Help" category—one of them lists 176,911 titles, the other lists 148,373. Those numbers include popular books, e-books, audio books, textbooks, podcasts, PDFs, and more—probably some duplicate copies of the same resource in various formats.

The point is not the exact number of self-help resources in print (the number changes daily), but the impressive, overall size of these offerings. Based on the assumption that publishers only produce resources that the public is buying, a lot of people in the world are looking for "help" on a variety of topics! Both the online resources cited break their "Self-Help" categories down into nearly 20 subcategories, covering the breadth of human experience.

There is one book of answers to life's questions that is set apart from all the rest: the Bible. Consider the author— God Himself. When God gives answers to our questions, it is like the watchmaker offering advice on how to use a watch he personally made. The one who created the watch knows the conditions in which it will perform best and knows how to re-set it should it lose its calibration.

No human author in the world can bring a "creator's" answers to life's deepest questions like God can. After all, He created every person and knows our deepest needs. He knows what He created us to be and how we can get there.

Almost all the books in the "Self-Help" fields are specialized—they focus on a narrow segment of life: dieting, marriage, self-esteem, depression, and others. But the Bible touches nearly every area of human existence and the questions that arise in those areas—all in one book!

Finally, the Bible is different because it is really not a self-help book—it is a "God-Help" book. God knows our fallen condition as human beings; He doesn't expect us to be able to answer life's questions on our own. Instead, He has revealed Himself to us through the Living Word, Jesus Christ, and the written Word, the Bible. Through the mediating work of the Holy Spirit who dwells in every Christian, God reveals the answers in the Bible to us. When we come to God in prayer with our needs, part of God's answer is often insight on how to apply the answers contained in Scripture.

Where to Go in the Bible When . . . is not meant to replace the Bible as a guide to life's answers. Instead, it is a guide *to* the Bible—a resource that will help you discover the Bible's answers to life's most challenging questions. If you have ever felt discouraged, felt lonely or alone, felt grief at the loss of a loved one or friend, felt frustrated with a persistent bad habit, felt insecure about your salvation, felt confused because you don't think God is hearing your prayers . . . then this resource will help.

Where to Go in the Bible When . . . is the ultimate Scripture guide—like a Bible concordance that is focused on common questions and felt needs about life. Overall, this resource is divided into sections that will help you quickly narrow your search and find God's answers: questions about God, about faith and the spiritual life, about other life issues such as finances, marriage, raising children, vocation, and relationships.

The world, including you, has questions. Let the Bible be your source for the answers. And let *Where to Go in the Bible When* . . . be your guide to the Bible.

Table of Contents

Emotions 52

Resources from Dr. David Jeremiah   266

WHERE

TO GO

IN THE

BIBLE

WHEN

...

Your Word I have

hidden in my heart,

That I might not sin

against You.

PSALM 119:11

Adversity

When facing an illness

Bless the Lord, O my soul,
And forget not all His benefits:
Who forgives all your iniquities,
Who heals all your diseases.

Psalm 103:2-3

Is anyone among you sick?
Let him call for the elders of the church,
And let them pray over him,
Anointing him with oil
In the name of the Lord.
And the prayer of faith will save the sick,
And the Lord will raise him up.
And if he has committed sins,
He will be forgiven.

James 5:14-15

God is my strength and power,
And He makes my way perfect.

2 Samuel 22:33

Give ear, O Lord, to my prayer;
And attend to the voice of my supplications.
In the day of my trouble I will call upon You,
For You will answer me.

Psalm 88:6-7

I will lift up my eyes to the hills—
From whence comes my help?
My help comes from the Lord,
Who made heaven and earth.
He will not allow your foot to be moved;
He who keeps you will not slumber.
Behold, He who keeps Israel
Shall neither slumber nor sleep.
The Lord is your keeper;
The Lord is your shade at your right hand.
The sun shall not strike you by day,
Nor the moon by night.

Psalm 121:1-6

The Lord is near to
all who call upon Him,
To all who call upon
Him in truth.

Psalm 145:18

Adversity

When concerned about finances

Therefore do not worry, saying, "What shall we eat?" or "What shall we drink?" or "What shall we wear?" For after all these things the Gentiles seek. For your heavenly Father knows that you need all these things.

Matthew 6:31-32

And my God shall supply all your need according to His riches in glory by Christ Jesus.

Philippians 4:19

He shall regard the prayer of the destitute, And shall not despise their prayer.

Psalm 102:17

The young lions lack and suffer hunger; But those who seek the Lord Shall not lack any good thing.

Psalm 34:10

Trust in the Lord, and do good;
Dwell in the land,
And feed on His faithfulness.
Delight yourself also in the Lord,
And He shall give you
The desires of your heart.

Psalm 37:3-4

For the Lord God is a sun and shield;
The Lord will give grace and glory;
No good thing will He withhold
From those who walk uprightly.

Psalm 84:11

When you have lost your job

Then Job arose, tore his robe, and shaved his head;
And he fell to the ground and worshiped.
And he said: "Naked I came from my mother's
womb, And naked shall I return there.
The Lord gave, and the Lord has taken away;
Blessed be the name of the Lord."
In all this Job did not sin nor charge God with wrong.

Job 1:20-22

Not that I speak in regard to need, for I have learned in whatever state I am, to be content: I know how to be abased, and I know how to abound. Everywhere and in all things I have learned both to be full and to be hungry, both to abound and to suffer need. I can do all things through Christ who strengthens me.

Philippians 4:11-13

A little that a righteous man has
Is better than the riches of many wicked.
For the arms of the wicked shall be broken,
But the Lord upholds the righteous.
The Lord knows the days of the upright,
And their inheritance shall be forever.
They shall not be ashamed in the evil time,
And in the days of famine they shall be satisfied.

Psalm 37:16-19

When you have no home

The Lord upholds all who fall,
And raises up all who
are bowed down.

Psalm 145:14

The righteous cry out, and the Lord hears,
And delivers them out of all their troubles.
The Lord is near to those who have a broken heart,
And saves such as have a contrite spirit.
Many are the afflictions of the righteous,
But the Lord delivers him out of them all.
He guards all his bones;
Not one of them is broken.

Psalm 34:17-20

Let not your heart be troubled;
You believe in God,
Believe also in Me.
In My Father's house
Are many mansions;
If it were not so,
I would have told you.
I go to prepare a place for you.
And if I go and prepare a place for you,
I will come again
And receive you to Myself;
That where I am,
There you may be also.

John 14:1-3

Adversity

When you're being attacked by Satan

Finally, my brethren, be strong in the Lord and in the power of His might. Put on the whole armor of God, that you may be able to stand against the wiles of the devil. For we do not wrestle against flesh and blood, but against principalities, against powers, against the rulers of the darkness of this age, against spiritual hosts of wickedness in the heavenly places. Therefore take up the whole armor of God, that you may be able to withstand in the evil day, and having done all, to stand.

Stand therefore, having girded your waist with truth, having put on the breastplate of righteousness, And having shod your feet with the preparation of the gospel of peace; above all, taking the shield of faith with which you will be able to quench all the fiery darts of the wicked one. And take the helmet of salvation, and the sword of the Spirit, which is the word of God; praying always with all prayer and supplication in the Spirit, being watchful to this end with all perseverance and supplication for all the saints.

Ephesians 6:10-18

As God lives, who has taken away my justice,
And the Almighty, who has made my soul bitter,
As long as my breath is in me,
And the breath of God in my nostrils,
My lips will not speak wickedness,
Nor my tongue utter deceit.
Far be it from me
That I should say you are right;
Till I die I will not put away my integrity from me.
My righteousness I hold fast, and will not let it go;
My heart shall not reproach me as long as I live.

Job 27:2-6

Watch, stand fast in the faith, be brave, be strong.

1 Corinthians 16:13

Be sober, be vigilant; because your adversary
the devil walks about like a roaring lion,
seeking whom he may devour.

1 Peter 5:8

Fight the good fight of faith, lay hold on eternal life,
to which you were also called and have confessed the
good confession in the presence of many witnesses.

1 Timothy 6:12

Adversity

For where two or three are gathered together
in My name, I am there in the midst of them.

Matthew 18:20

How you are fallen from heaven,
O Lucifer, son of the morning!
How you are cut down to the ground,
You who weakened the nations!
For you have said in your heart:
"I will ascend into heaven,
I will exalt my throne above the stars of God;
I will also sit on the mount of the congregation
On the farthest sides of the north;
I will ascend above the heights of the clouds,
I will be like the Most High."
Yet you shall be brought down to Sheol,
To the lowest depths of the Pit.
Those who see you will gaze at you,
And consider you, saying:
"Is this the man who made the earth tremble,
Who shook kingdoms,
Who made the world as a wilderness
And destroyed its cities,
Who did not open the house of his prisoners?"

Isaiah 14:12-17

Therefore gird up the loins of your mind, be sober, and rest your hope fully upon the grace that is to be brought to you at the revelation of Jesus Christ; as obedient children, not conforming yourselves to the former lusts, as in your ignorance; but as He who called you is holy, you also be holy in all your conduct, because it is written, "Be holy, for I am holy."

1 Peter 1:13-16

Then Jesus was led up by the Spirit into the wilderness to be tempted by the devil. And when He had fasted forty days and forty nights, afterward He was hungry. Now when the tempter came to Him, he said, "If You are the Son of God, command that these stones become bread."

But He answered and said, "It is written, 'Man shall not live by bread alone, but by every word that proceeds from the mouth of God.'"

Then the devil took Him up into the holy city, set Him on the pinnacle of the temple,

and said to Him, "If You are the Son of God,
throw Yourself down. For it is written:

'He shall give His angels charge over you,'
and,
'In their hands they shall bear you up,
Lest you dash your foot against a stone.'"

Jesus said to him, "It is written again,
'You shall not tempt the Lord your God.'"

Again, the devil took Him up on an exceedingly
high mountain, and showed Him all the
kingdoms of the world and their glory. And he
said to Him, "All these things I will give You
if You will fall down and worship me."

Then Jesus said to him, "Away with you, Satan!
For it is written, 'You shall worship the Lord
your God, and Him only you shall serve.'"

Then the devil left Him, and behold,
angels came and ministered to Him.

Matthew 4:1-11

Look to Me, and be saved,
All you ends of the earth!
For I am God, and there is no other.

Isaiah 45:22

My son, if you receive my words,
And treasure my commands within you,
So that you incline your ear to wisdom,
And apply your heart to understanding;
Yes, if you cry out for discernment,
And lift up your voice for understanding,
If you seek her as silver,
And search for her as for hidden treasures;
Then you will understand the fear of the Lord,
And find the knowledge of God.
For the Lord gives wisdom;
From His mouth come knowledge
and understanding;
He stores up sound wisdom for the upright;
He is a shield to those who walk uprightly;
He guards the paths of justice,
And preserves the way of His saints.

Proverbs 2:1-8

Adversity

He has delivered us from the power of darkness
and conveyed us into the kingdom of the Son
of His love, in whom we have redemption
through His blood, the forgiveness of sins.

Colossians 1:13-14

Therefore submit to God. Resist the
devil and he will flee from you.

James 4:7

Therefore, putting away lying, "Let each one
of you speak truth with his neighbor," for we
are members of one another. "Be angry, and
do not sin": do not let the sun go down on
your wrath, nor give place to the devil.

Ephesians 4:25-27

Therefore, in all things He had to be made like His
brethren, that He might be a merciful and faithful
High Priest in things pertaining to God, to make
propitiation for the sins of the people.
For in that He Himself has suffered, being
tempted, He is able to aid those who are tempted.

Hebrews 2:17-18

No temptation has overtaken you except such as
is common to man; but God is faithful, who will
not allow you to be tempted beyond what you are
able, but with the temptation will also make the
way of escape, that you may be able to bear it.

1 Corinthians 10:13

These things I have spoken to you, that
in Me you may have peace. In the world
you will have tribulation; but be of good
cheer, I have overcome the world."

John 16:33

Cast your burden on the Lord,
And He shall sustain you;
He shall never permit the righteous to be moved.

Psalm 55:22

Be anxious for nothing, but in everything by prayer
and supplication, with thanksgiving, let your
requests be made known to God; and the peace of
God, which surpasses all understanding, will guard
your hearts and minds through Christ Jesus.

Philippians 4:6-7

Adversity

Pursue peace with all people, and holiness,
without which no one will see the Lord:

Hebrews 12:14

When someone's words have hurt you

A soft answer turns away wrath,
But a harsh word stirs up anger.

Proverbs 15:1

But I say to you, love your enemies, bless those
who curse you, do good to those who hate you,
and pray for those who spitefully use you and
persecute you, that you may be sons of your Father
in heaven; for He makes His sun rise on the evil and
on the good, and sends rain on the just and on the
unjust. For if you love those who love you, what
reward have you? Do not even the tax collectors
do the same? And if you greet your brethren only,
what do you do more than others? Do not even
the tax collectors do so? Therefore you shall be
perfect, just as your Father in heaven is perfect.

Matthew 5:44-48

Bless those who persecute you; bless and do not curse.

Romans 12:14

The hypocrite with his mouth
destroys his neighbor,
But through knowledge the
righteous will be delivered.

Proverbs 11:9

Moreover if your brother sins against you,
Go and tell him his fault between you and him alone.
If he hears you, you have gained your brother.
But if he will not hear,
Take with you one or two more,
That "by the mouth of two or three witnesses
Every word may be established."
And if he refuses to hear them,
Tell it to the church.
But if he refuses even to hear the church,
Let him be to you like a heathen and a tax collector.

Matthew 18:15-17

Adversity

But why do you judge your brother?
Or why do you show contempt for your brother?
For we shall all stand before
the judgment seat of Christ.
For it is written: "As I live," says the Lord,
"Every knee shall bow to Me,
And every tongue shall confess to God."
So then each of us shall give
account of himself to God.

Romans 14:10-12

The Lord is near to those who have a broken heart,
And saves such as have a contrite spirit.

Psalm 34:18

When your enemies surround you

Though I walk in the midst of trouble,
You will revive me;
You will stretch out Your hand
Against the wrath of my enemies,
And Your right hand will save me.

Psalm 138:7

Make haste, O God, to deliver me!
Make haste to help me, O Lord!
Let them be ashamed and confounded
Who seek my life;
Let them be turned back and confused
Who desire my hurt.
Let them be turned back because of their shame,
Who say, "Aha, aha!"
Let all those who seek You rejoice and be glad in You;
And let those who love
Your salvation say continually,
"Let God be magnified!"
But I am poor and needy;
Make haste to me, O God!
You are my help and my deliverer;
O Lord, do not delay.

Psalm 70

For You are my rock and my fortress;
Therefore, for Your name's sake,
Lead me and guide me.
Pull me out of the net which they
have secretly laid for me,

Adversity

For You are my strength.
Into Your hand I commit my spirit;
You have redeemed me, O Lord God of truth.

Psalm 31:3-5

And Moses said to the people,
"Do not be afraid. Stand still,
And see the salvation of the Lord,
Which He will accomplish for you today.
For the Egyptians whom you see today,
You shall see again no more forever.
The Lord will fight for you,
And you shall hold your peace."

Exodus 14:13-14

You have heard that it was said, "You shall love
your neighbor and hate your enemy." But I say to
you, "Love your enemies, bless those who curse
you, do good to those who hate you, and pray for
those who spitefully use you and persecute you,
that you may be sons of your Father in heaven; for
He makes His sun rise on the evil and on the good,
and sends rain on the just and on the unjust."

Matthew 5:43-45

Then David said to the Philistine, "You come to
me with a sword, with a spear, and with a javelin.
But I come to you in the name of the Lord of hosts,
the God of the armies of Israel, whom you have
defied. This day the Lord will deliver you into
my hand, and I will strike you and take your head
from you. And this day I will give the carcasses of
the camp of the Philistines to the birds of the air
and the wild beasts of the earth, that all the earth
may know that there is a God in Israel. Then all
this assembly shall know that the Lord does not
save with sword and spear; for the battle is the
Lord's, and He will give you into our hands."

1 Samuel 17:45-47

When you've been misunderstood

Don't copy the behavior and customs of this world,
but let God transform you into a new person
by changing the way you think. Then you will know
what God wants you to do, and you will know how
good and pleasing and perfect His will really is.

Romans 12:2 (NLT)

Do not waste time arguing over godless ideas
and old wives' tales. Spend your time and energy
in training yourself for spiritual fitness.

1 Timothy 6:7 (NLT)

But the very hairs of your head are all
numbered. Do not fear therefore; you are
of more value than many sparrows.

Luke 12:7

Lord, You have searched me and known me.
You know my sitting down and my rising up;
You understand my thought afar off.
You comprehend my path and my lying down,
And are acquainted with all my ways.
For there is not a word on my tongue,
But behold, O Lord, You know it altogether.
You have hedged me behind and before,
And laid Your hand upon me.
Such knowledge is too wonderful for me;
It is high, I cannot attain it.

Psalm 139:1-6

When you need patience

For you have need of endurance, so that
after you have done the will of God,
you may receive the promise:
For yet a little while, and He who is
coming will come and will not tarry.
Now the just shall live by faith; but if anyone
draws back, my soul has no pleasure in him.

Hebrews 10:36-38

But the fruit of the Spirit is love, joy, peace,
longsuffering, kindness, goodness, faithfulness,
gentleness, self-control. Against such there is no law.

Galatians 5:22-23

Knowing that the testing of your faith produces
patience. But let patience have its perfect work, that
you may be perfect and complete, lacking nothing.

James 1:3-4

Therefore be patient, brethren, until the coming
of the Lord. See how the farmer waits for the
precious fruit of the earth, waiting patiently
for it until it receives the early and latter rain.
You also be patient. Establish your hearts,
for the coming of the Lord is at hand.

James 5:7-8

Indeed we count them blessed who endure.
You have heard of the perseverance of Job and
seen the end intended by the Lord—that the
Lord is very compassionate and merciful.

James 5:11

But He knows the way that I take;
When He has tested me, I shall come forth as gold.

Job 23:10

For when God made a promise to Abraham, because
He could swear by no one greater, He swore by
Himself, saying, "Surely blessing I will bless you,
and multiplying I will multiply you." And so, after
he had patiently endured, he obtained the promise.

Hebrews 6:13-15

The Lord is not slack concerning His promise,
as some count slackness, but is longsuffering
toward us, not willing that any should perish
but that all should come to repentance.

2 Peter 3:9

For this reason we also, since the day we heard it,
do not cease to pray for you, and to ask that you
may be filled with the knowledge of His will in
all wisdom and spiritual understanding; that you
may walk worthy of the Lord, fully pleasing Him,
being fruitful in every good work and increasing
in the knowledge of God; strengthened with all
might, according to His glorious power, for all
patience and longsuffering with joy; giving thanks
to the Father who has qualified us to be partakers
of the inheritance of the saints in the light.

Colossians 1:9-12

Adversity

He who is slow to anger is better than the mighty,
And he who rules his spirit than he who takes a city.

Proverbs 16:32

Whoever has no rule over his own spirit
Is like a city broken down, without walls.

Proverbs 25:28

I waited patiently
for the Lord;
And He inclined to me.
He also brought
me up out of a
horrible pit,
Out of the miry clay,
And set my feet upon a rock
and established my steps.

Psalm 40:1-2

Now may the God of patience and comfort
grant you to be like-minded toward one
another, according to Christ Jesus.

Romans 15:5

When a loved one has died

For if we live, we live to the Lord;
and if we die, we die to the Lord.
Therefore, whether we live or die, we are the Lord's.

Romans 14:8

Precious in the sight of the Lord
is the death of His saints.

Psalm 116:15

For God did not appoint us to wrath, but to obtain
salvation through our Lord Jesus Christ,
Who died for us, that whether we wake or
sleep, we should live together with Him.

1 Thessalonians 5:9-10

And God will wipe away every tear from their eyes;
there shall be no more death, nor sorrow, nor crying.
There shall be no more pain, for the
former things have passed away.

Revelation 21:4

Adversity

Yea, though I walk through
The valley of the shadow of death,
I will fear no evil;
For You are with me;
Your rod and Your staff,
They comfort me.

Psalm 23:4

Let not your heart be troubled;
You believe in God, believe also in Me.
In My Father's house are many mansions;
If it were not so, I would have told you.
I go to prepare a place for you.
And if I go and prepare a place for you,
I will come again and receive you to Myself;
That where I am, there you may be also.
And where I go you know, and the way you know.
Thomas said to Him, "Lord, we do not know
Where You are going, and how can
we know the way?"
Jesus said to him,
"I am the way, the truth, and the life.
No one comes to the Father except through Me.

John 14:1-6

When a child dies

Blessed are those who mourn,
For they shall be comforted.

Matthew 5:4

Watch, stand fast in the faith,
Be brave, be strong.

1 Corinthians 16:13

The name of the LORD *is* a strong tower;
The righteous run to it and are safe.

Proverbs 18:10

The LORD will command
His lovingkindness in the daytime,
And in the night His song shall
Be with me—a prayer to the God of my life.

Psalm 42:10

So the ransomed of the Lord shall return,
And come to Zion with singing,
With everlasting joy on their heads.
They shall obtain joy and gladness;
Sorrow and sighing shall flee away.

Isaiah 51:11

Adversity

Then his servants said to him, "What is this
that you have done? You fasted and wept
for the child while he was alive, but when
the child died, you arose and ate food."

And he said, "While the child was alive, I fasted
and wept; for I said, 'Who can tell whether
the Lord will be gracious to me, that the child
may live?' But now he is dead; why should I
fast? Can I bring him back again? I shall go
to him, but he shall not return to me."

2 Samuel 12:21-23

When the world frightens you

He makes wars cease to the end of the earth;
He breaks the bow and cuts the spear in two;
He burns the chariot in the fire.
Be still, and know that I am God;
I will be exalted among the nations,
I will be exalted in the earth!
The Lord of hosts is with us;
The God of Jacob is our refuge.

Psalm 46:9-11

These things I have spoken to you, that
in Me you may have peace. In the world
you will have tribulation; but be of good
cheer, I have overcome the world.

John 16:33

Who has measured the waters
In the hollow of His hand,
Measured heaven with a span
And calculated the dust of the
Earth in a measure?
Weighed the mountains in scales
And the hills in a balance?
Who has directed the Spirit of the Lord,
Or as His counselor has taught Him?
With whom did He take counsel,
And who instructed Him,
And taught Him in the path of justice?
Who taught Him knowledge,
And showed Him the way of understanding?
Behold, the nations are as a drop in a bucket,
And are counted as the small dust on the scales;
Look, He lifts up the isles as a very little thing.

Isaiah 40:12-15

Adversity

Come to Me, all you who labor and are heavy laden, and I will give you rest. Take My yoke upon you and learn from Me, for I am gentle and lowly in heart, and you will find rest for your souls. For My yoke is easy and My burden is light.

Matthew 11:28-30

When miles separate you from a loved one

Be anxious for nothing, but in everything by prayer and supplication, with thanksgiving, let your requests be made known to God; and the peace of God, which surpasses all understanding, will guard your hearts and minds through Christ Jesus.

Philippians 4:6-7

If then you were raised with Christ, seek those things which are above, where Christ is, sitting at the right hand of God. Set your mind on things above, not on things on the earth.

Colossians 3:1-2

For our citizenship is in heaven, from which we also
eagerly wait for the Savior, the Lord Jesus Christ.

Philippians 3:20

But seek first the kingdom of God
and His righteousness, and all these
things shall be added to you.

Matthew 6:33

Great peace have those who love Your law,
And nothing causes them to stumble.

Psalm 119:165

Of old You laid the foundation of the earth,
And the heavens are the work of Your hands.
They will perish, but You will endure;
Yes, they will all grow old like a garment;
Like a cloak You will change them,
And they will be changed.
But You are the same,
And Your years will have no end.
The children of Your servants will continue,
And their descendants will be established before You.

Psalm 102:25-28

Adversity

Casting all your care upon Him, for He cares for you.

1 Peter 5:7

For though I am absent in the flesh,
yet I am with you in spirit,
Rejoicing to see your good order and the
steadfastness of your faith in Christ.

Colossians 2:5

A friend loves at all times,
And a brother is born for adversity.

Proverbs 17:17

When you just need to be comforted

And we know that all things
work together for good
to those who love God,
To those who are the called
according to His purpose.

Romans 8:28

Blessed be the God and Father
of our Lord Jesus Christ,
The Father of mercies and God of all comfort,
who comforts us in all our tribulation, that
we may be able to comfort those who are in
any trouble, with the comfort with which
we ourselves are comforted by God.

2 Corinthians 1:3-4

Now may our Lord Jesus Christ Himself,
and our God and Father, who has loved us
and given us everlasting consolation and
good hope by grace, comfort your hearts and
establish you in every good word and work.

2 Thessalonians 2:16-17

Come to me, all you who labor and are
heavy laden, and I will give you rest.
Take my yoke upon you and learn from me,
for I am gentle and lowly in heart,
and you will find rest for your souls.

Matthew 11:28-29

Adversity

THE NAME OF THE LORD

IS A STRONG TOWER;

THE RIGHTEOUS RUN TO IT

AND ARE SAFE.

PSALM 18:17

Emotions

When you are unhappy

He who heeds the word wisely will find good,
And whoever trusts in the Lord, happy is he.

Proverbs 16:20

The Lord is far from the wicked,
But He hears the prayer of the righteous.

Proverbs 15:29

If you keep My commandments, You will abide in My
love, just as I have kept My Father's Commandments
and abide in His love. These things I have spoken
to you, that My joy may remain in you, and that
your joy may be full. This is My commandment,
that you love one another as I have loved you.

John 15:10-12

But the fruit of the Spirit is love, joy, peace,
longsuffering, kindness, goodness, faithfulness,
gentleness, self-control. Against such there is no law.

Galatians 5:22-23

Commit your works to the Lord and
your thoughts will be established.

Proverbs 16:3

Anxiety in the heart of man causes depression,
But a good word makes it glad.

Proverbs 12:25

Then he said to them, "Go your way, eat
the fat, drink the sweet, and send portions
to those for whom nothing is prepared; for
this day is holy to our Lord. Do not sorrow,
for the joy of the Lord is your strength."

Nehemiah 8:10

When you need help praising

I will bless the Lord at all times;
His praise shall continually be in my mouth.

Psalm 34:1

Oh, the depth of the riches both of the wisdom
and knowledge of God! How unsearchable are His
judgments and His ways past finding out!

"For who has known the mind of the Lord?
Or who has become His counselor?"
"Or who has first given to Him
And it shall be repaid to him?"
For of Him and through Him and to Him are
all things, to whom be glory forever. Amen.

Romans 11:33-36

Behold, God is great, and we do not know Him;
Nor can the number of His years be discovered.

Job 36:22-26

Both riches and honor come from You,
And You reign over all.
In Your hand is power and might;
In Your hand it is to make great
And to give strength to all.
Now therefore, our God,
We thank You
And praise Your glorious name.

1 Chronicles 29:12-13

Behold, God is exalted by His power;
Who teaches like Him?
Who has assigned Him His way,
Or who has said, 'You have done wrong'?
Remember to magnify His work,
Of which men have sung.
Everyone has seen it;
Man looks on it from afar.

Job 36:22-26

The Lord lives!
Blessed be my Rock!
Let God be exalted,
The Rock of my salvation!

2 Samuel 22:47

Let the heavens rejoice, and let the earth be glad;
And let them say among the nations,
"The Lord reigns."
Let the sea roar, and all its fullness;
Let the field rejoice, and all that is in it.
Then the trees of the woods shall
rejoice before the Lord,
For He is coming to judge the earth.

1 Chronicles 16:31-33

Emotions

Sing to the Lord, all the earth;
Proclaim the good news of His
salvation from day to day.
Declare His glory among the nations,
His wonders among all peoples.
For the Lord is great and greatly to be praised;
He is also to be feared above all gods.

1 Chronicles 16:23-25

For I proclaim the name of the Lord:
Ascribe greatness to our God.
He is the Rock, His work is perfect;
For all His ways are justice,
A God of truth and without injustice;
Righteous and upright is He.

Deuteronomy 32:3-4

Yet I will rejoice in the Lord,
I will joy in the God of my salvation.
The Lord God is my strength;
He will make my feet like deer's feet,
And He will make me walk on my high hills.

Habakkuk 3:18-19

I will sing to the Lord,
Because He has dealt bountifully with me.

Psalm 13:6

Daniel answered and said:

Blessed be the name of God forever and ever,
For wisdom and might are His.
And He changes the times and the seasons;
He removes kings and raises up kings;
He gives wisdom to the wise
And knowledge to those who have understanding.
He reveals deep and secret things;
He knows what is in the darkness,
And light dwells with Him.

I thank You and praise You,
O God of my fathers;
You have given me wisdom and might,
And have now made known to me
what we asked of You.

Daniel 2:20-23

Emotions

Sing to the Lord a new song,
And His praise from the ends of the earth,
You who go down to the sea, and all that is in it,
You coastlands and you inhabitants of them!
Let the wilderness and its cities lift up their voice,
The villages that Kedar inhabits.
Let the inhabitants of Sela sing,
Let them shout from the top of the mountains.
Let them give glory to the Lord,
And declare His praise in the coastlands.

Isaiah 42:10-12

Oh, clap your hands, all you peoples!
Shout to God with the voice of triumph!
For the Lord Most High is awesome;
He is a great King over all the earth.

Psalm 47:1-2

Let the word of Christ dwell in you richly in
all wisdom, teaching and admonishing one
another in psalms and hymns and spiritual songs,
singing with grace in your hearts to the Lord.

Colossians 3:16

Therefore by Him let us continually offer the
sacrifice of praise to God, that is, the fruit
of our lips, giving thanks to His name.

Hebrews 13:15

I will praise You with my whole heart;
Before the gods I will sing praises to You.
I will worship toward Your holy temple,
And praise Your name
For Your lovingkindness and Your truth;
For You have magnified Your word above
all Your name.
In the day when I cried out, You answered me,
And made me bold with strength in my soul.
All the kings of the earth shall praise You, O Lord,
When they hear the words of Your mouth.
Yes, they shall sing of the ways of the Lord,
For great is the glory of the Lord.
Though the Lord is on high,
Yet He regards the lowly;
But the proud He knows from afar.

Psalm 138

Whoever offers praise glorifies Me;
And to him who orders his conduct aright
I will show the salvation of God.

Psalm 50:23

It is good to give thanks to the Lord,
And to sing praises to Your name, O Most High.

Psalm 92:1

Make a joyful shout to the Lord, all you lands!
Serve the Lord with gladness;
Come before His presence with singing.
Know that the Lord, He is God;
It is He who has made us, and not we ourselves;
We are His people and the sheep of His pasture.
Enter into His gates with thanksgiving,
And into His courts with praise.
Be thankful to Him, and bless His name.
For the Lord is good;
His mercy is everlasting,
And His truth endures to all generations.

Psalm 100

Oh, that men would give thanks to the Lord
for His goodness,
And for His wonderful works to the children of men!

Psalm 107:8

I will praise You, for I am fearfully
and wonderfully made;
Marvelous are Your works,
And that my soul knows very well.

Psalm 139:14

Therefore by Him let us continually offer the
sacrifice of praise to God, that is, the fruit
of our lips, giving thanks to His name.

Hebrews 13:15

When temptation overcomes you

For in that He Himself has suffered, being tempted,
He is able to aid those who are tempted.

Hebrews 2:18

You are my hiding place and my shield;
I hope in Your word.

Psalm 119:114

Emotions

My brethren, count it all joy when you fall
into various trials, knowing that the testing
of your faith produces patience. But let
patience have its perfect work, that you may
be perfect and complete, lacking nothing.

James 1:2-4

Blessed is the man who endures temptation;
for when he has been approved, He will
receive the crown of life which the Lord
has promised to those who love Him.

James 1:12

Then the Lord knows how to deliver the godly
out of temptations, and to reserve the unjust
under punishment for the day of judgment.

2 Peter 2:9

No temptation has overtaken you except such as
is common to man; but God is faithful, who will
not allow you to be tempted beyond what you are
able, but with the temptation will also make the
way of escape, that you may be able to bear it.

1 Corinthians 10:13

The Lord shall preserve you from evil;
He shall preserve your soul,
The Lord shall preserve your
going out and coming in
From this time forth and ever forevermore.

Psalm 121:7-8

When fear cripples you

God is our refuge and strength,
A very present help in trouble.
Therefore we will not fear,
Even though the earth be removed,
And though the mountains be carried
Into the midst of the sea;

Psalm 46:1-2

Direct my steps by Your word,
And let no iniquity have dominion over me.

Psalm 119:133

Peace I leave with you, My peace I give to you;
not as the world gives do I give to you. Let not
your heart be troubled, neither let it be afraid.

John 14:27

Emotions

The Lord is my light and my salvation;
Whom shall I fear?
The Lord is the strength of my life;
Of whom shall I be afraid?

Psalm 27:1

But now, thus says the Lord,
Who created you, O Jacob,
And He who formed you, O Israel:
"Fear not, for I have redeemed you;
I have called you by your name;
You are Mine.
When you pass through the waters,
I will be with you;
And through the rivers,
they shall not overflow you.
When you walk through the fire,
you shall not be burned,
Nor shall the flame scorch you.
For I am the Lord your God,
The Holy One of Israel, your Savior.

Isaiah 43:1-3a

I, even I, am He who comforts you.
Who are you that you should be afraid
of a man who will die,
And of the son of a man who will be made like grass?

Isaiah 51:12

Wait on the Lord;
Be of good courage,
And He shall strengthen your heart;
Wait, I say, on the Lord!

Psalm 27:14

In God I have put my trust;
I will not be afraid.
What can man do to me?

Psalm 56:11

There is no fear in love; but perfect love casts out
fear, because fear involves torment.
But he who fears has not been made perfect in love.

1 John 4:18

Emotions

When anxiety hinders you

My eyes are awake through the night watches,
That I may meditate on Your word.
Hear my voice according to Your lovingkindness
O Lord revive me according to your justice.

Psalm 119:148-149

You will keep him in perfect peace,
Whose mind is stayed on You,
Because he trusts in You.

Isaiah 26:3

These things I have spoken to you,
That in Me you may have peace.
In the world you will have tribulation;
But be of good cheer, I have overcome the world.

John 16:33

Come to Me, all you who labor
And are heavy laden, and I will give you rest.
Take My yoke upon you and learn from Me,
For I am gentle and lowly in heart,
And you will find rest for your souls.
For My yoke is easy and My burden is light.

Matthew 11:28-30

Be anxious for nothing, but in everything by
prayer and supplication, with thanksgiving, let
your requests be made known to God; and the
peace of God, which surpasses all understanding,
will guard your hearts and minds through
Christ Jesus.

Philippians 4:6-7

I will both lie down in peace, and sleep;
For You alone, O Lord, make me dwell in safety.

Psalm 4:8

Therefore, having been justified by faith, we have
peace with God through our Lord Jesus Christ,
through whom also we have access by faith into this
grace in which we stand, and rejoice in hope of the
glory of God. And not only that, but we also glory
in tribulations, knowing that tribulation produces
perseverance; and perseverance, character; and
character, hope. Now hope does not disappoint,
because the love of God has been poured out in our
hearts by the Holy Spirit who was given to us.

Romans 5:1-5

Emotions

The Lord is my shepherd;
I shall not want.
He makes me to lie down in green pastures;
He leads me beside the still waters.
He restores my soul;
He leads me in the paths of righteousness
For His name's sake.

Psalm 23:1-3

The things which you learned and received
and heard and saw in me, these do, and
the God of peace will be with you.

Philippians 4:9

When jealousy controls you

Do not let your heart envy sinners, but be
zealous for the fear of the Lord all the day.

Proverbs 23:17

Let us walk properly, as in the day,
Not in revelry and drunkenness,
Not in lewdness and lust,
Not in strife and envy.

Romans 13:13

Do not fret because of those who are evil
Or be envious of those who do wrong;
For like the grass they will soon wither,
Like green plants they will soon die away.
Trust in the Lord and do good;
Dwell in the land and enjoy safe pasture.
Take delight in the Lord,
And he will give you the desires of your heart.
Commit your way to the Lord;
Trust in him and he will do this:
He will make your righteous reward shine
like the dawn,
Your vindication like the noonday sun.
Be still before the Lord
And wait patiently for him;
Do not fret when people succeed in their ways,
When they carry out their wicked schemes.

                                    Psalm 37:1-7 (NIV)

Let us not become conceited,
Provoking one another,
Envying one another.

                                    Galatians 5:26

Emotions

Let nothing be done through
selfish ambition or conceit,
But in lowliness of mind let
each esteem others better than himself.
Let each of you look out not only for his own
interests, but also for the interests of others.
Let this mind be in you which was also in Christ
Jesus, Who, being in the form of God,
Did not consider it robbery to be equal with God,
but made Himself of no reputation,
Taking the form of a bondservant, and
coming in the likeness of men.

Philippians 2:3-7

When helplessness drags you down

The angel of the Lord encamps
All around those who fear Him,
And delivers them.

Psalm 34:7

Let us therefore come boldly to the throne of grace,
That we may obtain mercy and find
grace to help in time of need.

Hebrews 4:16

Therefore humble yourselves under the mighty hand
of God, that He may exalt you in due time,
casting all your care upon Him, for He cares for you.
Be sober, be vigilant, because your adversary
the devil walks about like a roaring lion, seeking
whom he may devour. Resist him, steadfast in
the faith, knowing that the same sufferings are
experienced by your brotherhood in the world.

1 Peter 5:6-9

When doubt nags at you

Commit your way to the Lord,
Trust also in Him,
And He shall bring it to pass.

Psalm 37:5

Trust in the Lord with all your heart,
And lean not on your own understanding;
In all your ways acknowledge Him,
And He shall direct your paths.

Proverbs 3:5-6

But without faith it is impossible to please Him, for he who comes to God must believe that He is, and that He is a rewarder of those who diligently seek Him.

Hebrews 11:6

But let him ask in faith, with no doubting, for he who doubts is like a wave of the sea driven and tossed by the wind. For let not that man suppose that he will receive anything from the Lord; he is a double-minded man, unstable in all his ways.

James 1:6-8

"Come now, therefore, and I will send you to Pharaoh that you may bring My people, the children of Israel, out of Egypt."

But Moses said to God, "Who am I that I should go to Pharaoh, and that I should bring the children of Israel out of Egypt?"

So He said, "I will certainly be with you. And this shall be a sign to you that I have sent you: When you have brought the people out of Egypt, you shall serve God on this mountain."

Exodus 3:10-12

Now Thomas, called the Twin, one of the twelve,
was not with them when Jesus came.
The other disciples therefore said to him,
"We have seen the Lord."
So he said to them, "Unless I see in His hands the
print of the nails, And put my finger into the print
of the nails, And put my hand into His side,
I will not believe."
And after eight days His disciples were again inside,
and Thomas with them. Jesus came, the doors being
shut, and stood in the midst, and said, "Peace to you!"
Then He said to Thomas, "Reach your finger here,
and look at My hands; and reach your hand here,
and put it into My side.
Do not be unbelieving, but believing."
And Thomas answered and said to Him,
"My Lord and my God!"
Jesus said to him, "Thomas, because you have
seen Me, you have believed. Blessed are those
who have not seen and yet have believed."

John 20:24-29

For we walk by faith, not by sight.

2 Corinthians 5:7

Emotions

Gideon said to Him, "O my lord, if the Lord is with us, why then has all this happened to us? And where are all His miracles which our fathers told us about, saying, 'Did not the Lord bring us up from Egypt?' But now the Lord has forsaken us and delivered us into the hands of the Midianites."

Then the Lord turned to him and said, "Go in this might of yours, and you shall save Israel from the hand of the Midianites. Have I not sent you?"

So he said to Him, "O my Lord, how can I save Israel? Indeed my clan is the weakest in Manasseh, and I am the least in my father's house."

And the Lord said to him, "Surely I will be with you, and you shall defeat the Midianites as one man."

Judges 6:13-16

"For My thoughts are not your thoughts,
Nor are your ways My ways," says the Lord.
"For as the heavens are higher than the earth,
So are My ways higher than your ways,
And My thoughts than your thoughts."

Isaiah 55:8-9

Oh, the depth of the riches both of the wisdom and
knowledge of God! How unsearchable are
His judgments and His ways past finding out!
For who has known the mind of the Lord?
Or who has become His counselor?

Romans 11:33-34

When loneliness overwhelms you

When my father and my mother forsake me,
Then the Lord will take care of me.

Psalm 27:10

I would have lost heart, unless I believed
That I would see the goodness of the Lord
In the land of the living.
Wait on the Lord;
Be of good courage and He shall strengthen
Your heart;
Wait. I say, on the Lord!

Psalm 28:14

A man who has friends must himself be friendly,
But there is a friend who sticks closer than a brother.

Proverbs 18:24

You are My friends if you do
whatever I command you.

John 15:14

At my first defense no one stood with me, but all
forsook me. May it not be charged against them.
But the Lord stood with me and strengthened
me, so that the message might be preached fully
through me, and that all the Gentiles might hear.
Also I was delivered out of the mouth of the lion.
And the Lord will deliver me from every evil
work and preserve me for His heavenly kingdom.
To Him be glory forever and ever. Amen!

2 Timothy 4:16-18

The Lord your God in your midst,
The Mighty One, will save;
He will rejoice over you with gladness,
He will quiet you with His love,
He will rejoice over you with singing.

Zephaniah 3:17

Teaching them to observe all things that I
have commanded you; and lo, I am with you
always, even to the end of the age. Amen.

Matthew 28:20

The Lord is near to those who have a broken heart,
And saves such as have a contrite spirit.

Psalm 34:18

When my father and my mother forsake me,
Then the Lord will take care of me.

Psalm 27:10

When discouragement weakens you

Wait on the Lord;
Be of good courage,
And He shall strengthen your heart;
Wait, I say, on the Lord!

Psalm 27:14

Do not sorrow, for the joy of the
Lord is your strength.

Nehemiah 8:10b

Emotions

This Book of the Law shall
not depart from your mouth,
But you shall meditate in it day and night,
That you may observe to do according to
all that is written in it.
For then you will make your way prosperous,
And then you will have good success.
Have I not commanded you?
Be strong and of good courage;
Do not be afraid, nor be dismayed,
For the Lord your God is with you wherever you go.

Joshua 1:8-9

I sought the Lord, and He heard me,
And delivered me from all my fears.
They looked to Him and were radiant,
And their faces were not ashamed.
This poor man cried out,
And the Lord heard him,
And saved him out of all his troubles.
The angel of the Lord encamps
All around those who fear Him,
And delivers them.
Oh, taste and see that the Lord is good;
Blessed is the man who trusts in Him!

Psalm 34:4-8

Therefore you now have sorrow; but I will
see you again and your heart will rejoice,
and your joy no one will take from you.

John 16:22

The righteous cry out, and the Lord hears,
And delivers them out of all their troubles.
The Lord is near to those who have a broken heart,
And saves such as have a contrite spirit.
Many are the afflictions of the righteous,
But the Lord delivers him out of them all.

Psalm 34:17-19

Why are you cast down, O my soul?
And why are you disquieted within me?
Hope in God;
For I shall yet praise Him,
The help of my countenance and my God.

Psalm 43:5

Cast your burden on the Lord,
And He shall sustain you;
He shall never permit the righteous to be moved.

Psalm 55:22

Emotions

The Lord is my strength and my shield;
My heart trusted in Him, and I am helped;
Therefore my heart greatly rejoices,
And with my song I will praise Him.

Psalm 28:7

The Lord will give strength to His people;
The Lord will bless His people with peace.

Psalm 29:11

He gives power to the weak,
And to those who have no might
He increases strength.
Even the youths shall faint and be weary,
And the young men shall utterly fall,
But those who wait on the Lord
Shall renew their strength;
They shall mount up with wings like eagles,
They shall run and not be weary,
They shall walk and not faint.

Isaiah 40:29-31

When worry paralyzes you

Be anxious for nothing, but in everything by prayer and supplication, with thanksgiving, let your requests be made known to God; and the peace of God, which surpasses all understanding, will guard your hearts and minds through Christ Jesus.

Philippians 4:6-7

Therefore humble yourselves under the mighty hand of God, that He may exalt you in due time, casting all your care upon Him, for He cares for you.

1 Peter 5:6-7

He who did not spare His own Son, but delivered Him up for us all, how shall He not with Him also freely give us all things?

Romans 8:32

For I am persuaded that neither death nor life, nor angels nor principalities nor powers, nor things present nor things to come, nor height nor depth, nor any other created thing, shall be able to separate us from the love of God which is in Christ Jesus our Lord.

Romans 8:38-39

Therefore I say to you, do not worry about your life, what you will eat or what you will drink; nor about your body, what you will put on. Is not life more than food and the body more than clothing? Look at the birds of the air, for they neither sow nor reap nor gather into barns; yet your heavenly Father feeds them. Are you not of more value than they? Which of you by worrying can add one cubit to his stature?

So why do you worry about clothing? Consider the lilies of the field, how they grow: they neither toil nor spin; and yet I say to you that even Solomon in all his glory was not arrayed like one of these. Now if God so clothes the grass of the field, which today is, and tomorrow is thrown into the oven, will He not much more clothe you, O you of little faith?

Therefore do not worry, saying, "What shall we eat?" or "What shall we drink?" or "What shall we wear?" For after all these things the Gentiles seek. For your heavenly Father knows that you need all these things. But seek first the kingdom of God and His righteousness, and all these things shall be added to you. Therefore do not worry about tomorrow, for tomorrow will worry about its own things. Sufficient for the day is its own trouble.

Matthew 6:25-34

When I consider Your heavens,
the work of Your fingers,
The moon and the stars, which You have ordained,
What is man that You are mindful of him,
And the son of man that You visit him?
For You have made him a little lower than the angels,
And You have crowned him with glory and honor.
You have made him to have dominion
over the works of Your hands;
You have put all things under his feet,
All sheep and oxen—
Even the beasts of the field,
The birds of the air,
And the fish of the sea
That pass through the paths of the seas.

Psalm 8:3-8

No more shall every man teach his neighbor, and
every man his brother, saying, "Know the Lord,"
for they all shall know Me, from the least of them to
the greatest of them, says the Lord. For I will forgive
their iniquity, and their sin I will remember no more.

Jeremiah 31:34

Emotions

When anger rages within you

"Be angry, and do not sin": do not let
the sun go down on your wrath.

Ephesians 4:26

So then, my beloved brethren, let every man be swift
to hear, slow to speak, slow to wrath; for the wrath
of man does not produce the righteousness of God.

James 1:19-20

Therefore, laying aside all malice, all deceit,
hypocrisy, envy, and all evil speaking, as
newborn babes, desire the pure milk of the
word, that you may grow thereby.

1 Peter 2:1-2

Cease from anger, and forsake wrath;
Do not fret—it only causes harm.

Psalm 37:8

But now you yourselves are to put off all these:
Anger, wrath, malice, blasphemy,
Filthy language out of your mouth.

Colossians 3:8

But I say to you who hear: Love your enemies,
Do good to those who hate you,
Bless those who curse you,
And pray for those who spitefully use you.
To him who strikes you on the one cheek,
Offer the other also.
And from him who takes away your cloak,
Do not withhold your tunic either.
Give to everyone who asks of you.
And from him who takes away your goods
Do not ask them back.
And just as you want men to do to you,
You also do to them likewise.
But if you love those who love you,
What credit is that to you?
For even sinners love those who love them.
And if you do good to those who do good to you,
What credit is that to you?
For even sinners do the same.
And if you lend to those from whom
you hope to receive back,
What credit is that to you?
For even sinners lend to sinners to
receive as much back.

Emotions

But love your enemies, do good, and lend,
Hoping for nothing in return
and your reward will be great,
And you will be sons of the Most High.
For He is kind to the unthankful and evil.

Luke 6:27-35

If it is possible, as much as depends on you,
Live peaceably with all men.
Beloved, do not avenge yourselves,
But rather give place to wrath; for it is written,
"Vengeance is Mine, I will repay," says the Lord.
Therefore "If your enemy is hungry, feed him;
If he is thirsty, give him a drink;
For in so doing you will heap coals
of fire on his head."
Do not be overcome by evil, but
overcome evil with good.

Romans 12:18-21

Finally, all of you be of one mind,
Having compassion for one another;
Love as brothers, be tenderhearted, be courteous;
Not returning evil for evil or reviling for reviling,
But on the contrary blessing,
Knowing that you were called to this,
That you may inherit a blessing. For
"He who would love life
And see good days,
Let him refrain his tongue from evil,
And his lips from speaking deceit.
Let him turn away from evil and do good;
Let him seek peace and pursue it.
For the eyes of the Lord are on the righteous,
And His ears are open to their prayers;
But the face of the Lord is against those who do evil."

1 Peter 3:8-12

A soft answer turns away wrath,
But a harsh word stirs up anger.

Proverbs 15:1

Emotions

For God did not appoint us to wrath,
But to obtain salvation through
our Lord Jesus Christ,
Who died for us, that whether we wake or sleep,
We should live together with Him.
Therefore comfort each other
And edify one another,
Just as you also are doing.

1 Thessalonians 5:9-11

When failure taunts you

As a father pities his children,
So the Lord pities those who fear Him.
For He knows our frame;
He remembers that we are dust.

Psalm 103:13-14

Let us therefore come boldly to the throne
of grace, that we may obtain mercy and
find grace to help in time of need.

Hebrews 4:16

But we have this treasure in earthen vessels, that the excellence of the power may be of God and not of us. We are hard-pressed on every side, yet not crushed; we are perplexed, but not in despair; persecuted, but not forsaken; struck down, but not destroyed—always carrying about in the body the dying of the Lord Jesus, that the life of Jesus also may be manifested in our body. For we who live are always delivered to death for Jesus' sake, that the life of Jesus also may be manifested in our mortal flesh. So then death is working in us, but life in you.

And since we have the same spirit of faith, according to what is written, "I believed and therefore I spoke," we also believe and therefore speak, knowing that He who raised up the Lord Jesus will also raise us up with Jesus, and will present us with you. For all things are for your sakes, that grace, having spread through the many, may cause thanksgiving to abound to the glory of God.

Therefore we do not lose heart. Even though our outward man is perishing, yet the inward man is being renewed day by day. For our light affliction, which is but for a moment, is working

for us a far more exceeding and eternal weight of
glory, while we do not look at the things which
are seen, but at the things which are not seen.
For the things which are seen are temporary,
but the things which are not seen are eternal.

2 Corinthians 4:7-18

The Lord God is my strength;
He will make my feet like deer's feet,
And He will make me walk on my high hills.

Habakkuk 3:19

He has not dealt with us according to our sins,
Nor punished us according to our iniquities.

Psalm 103:10

Though he fall, he shall not be utterly cast down;
For the Lord upholds him with His hand.

Psalm 37:24

Being confident of this very thing, that He
who has begun a good work in you will
complete it until the day of Jesus Christ.

Philippians 1:6

In Him we have redemption through His blood,
the forgiveness of sins, according to the riches of
His grace which He made to abound toward us
in all wisdom and prudence, having made known
to us the mystery of His will, according to His
good pleasure which He purposed in Himself.

Ephesians 1:7-9

When you covet your neighbor's possessions

Let your conduct be without covetousness;
Be content with such things as you have.
For He Himself has said,
"I will never leave you nor forsake you."

Hebrews 13:5

And He said to them,
"Take heed and beware of covetousness,
for one's life does not consist in the
abundance of the things he possesses."

Luke 12:15

Emotions

For this you know, that no fornicator, unclean
person, nor covetous man, who is an idolater, has
any inheritance in the kingdom of Christ and God.

Ephesians 5:5

Where do wars and fights come from among you?
Do they not come from your desires for pleasure
That war in your members?
You lust and do not have.
You murder and covet and cannot obtain.
You fight and war. Yet you do not have
because you do not ask.
You ask and do not receive, because you ask amiss,
That you may spend it on your pleasures.
Adulterers and adulteresses!

Do you not know that friendship with
the world is enmity with God?

Whoever therefore wants to be a friend of the
world makes himself an enemy of God.

James 4:1-4

For the love of money is a root of all kinds
of evil, for which some have strayed from
the faith in their greediness, and pierced
themselves through with many sorrows.

1 Timothy 6:10

For what profit is it to a man
If he gains the whole world,
And loses his own soul?
Or what will a man give
In exchange for his soul?

Matthew 16:26

For the commandments,
"You shall not commit adultery,"
"You shall not murder," "You shall not steal,"
"You shall not bear false witness,"
"You shall not covet,"
And if there is any other commandment,
Are all summed up in this saying, namely,
"You shall love your neighbor as yourself."

Romans 13:9

Emotions

Do not love the world or the things in the world.
If anyone loves the world,
The love of the Father is not in him.
For all that is in the world—the lust of the flesh,
The lust of the eyes, and the pride of life—
Is not of the Father but is of the world.
And the world is passing away, and the lust of it;
But he who does the will of God abides forever.

1 John 2:15-17

Sell what you have and give alms;
Provide yourselves money bags
which do not grow old,
A treasure in the heavens that does not fail,
Where no thief approaches nor moth destroys.
For where your treasure is, there
your heart will be also.

Luke 12:33-34

When depression saddens you

Yea, though I walk through the valley
of the shadow of death,
I will fear no evil; For You are with me;
Your rod and Your staff, they comfort me.

Psalm 23:4

The Lord is near to those who have a broken
heart, and saves such as have a contrite spirit.

Psalm 34:18

I waited patiently for the Lord;
And He inclined to me,
And heard my cry.
He also brought me up out of a horrible pit,
Out of the miry clay,
And set my feet upon a rock,
And established my steps.
He has put a new song in my mouth—
Praise to our God;
Many will see it and fear,
And will trust in the Lord.

Psalm 40:1-3

Emotions

As for me I will call upon God
And the Lord shall save me.
Evening and morning and at noon
I will pray, and cry aloud,
And He shall hear my voice.
He has redeemed my soul in peace
From the battle that was against me,
For there were many against me.

Psalm 55:16-18

...To give light to those who sit
in darkness and the shadow of death,
to guide our feet into the way of peace.

Luke 1:79

Likewise the Spirit also helps in our weaknesses.
For we do not know what we should pray for as we
ought, but the Spirit Himself makes intercession
for us with groanings which cannot be uttered.
Now He who searches the hearts knows what the
mind of the Spirit is, because He makes intercession
for the saints according to the will of God.

Romans 8:26-27

Blessed is the man who trusts in the Lord,
And whose hope is the Lord.
For he shall be like a tree planted by the waters,
Which spreads out its roots by the river,
And will not fear when heat comes;
But its leaf will be green,
And will not be anxious in the year of drought,
Nor will cease from yielding fruit.

Jeremiah 17:7-8

The eternal God is your refuge,
And underneath are the everlasting arms;
He will thrust out the enemy from before you,
And will say, 'Destroy!'

Deuteronomy 33:27

Have I not commanded you? Be strong and of good
courage; do not be afraid, nor be dismayed, for the
Lord your God is with you wherever you go."

Joshua 1:9

From the end of the earth I will cry to You,
When my heart is overwhelmed;
Lead me to the rock that is higher than I.

Psalm 61:2

Emotions

When hopelessness drowns you

Why are you cast down, O my soul?
And why are you disquieted within me?
Hope in God;
For I shall yet praise Him,
The help of my countenance and my God.

Psalm 43:5

Surely goodness and mercy shall follow me
All the days of my life;
And I will dwell in the house of the Lord
Forever.

Psalm 23:6

And we know that all things work together
for good to those who love God, to those who
are the called according to His purpose.

Romans 8:28

But seek first the kingdom of God
and His righteousness, and all these
things shall be added to you.

Matthew 6:33

Blessed are the poor in spirit,
For theirs is the kingdom of heaven.
Blessed are those who mourn,
For they shall be comforted ...
Blessed are those who are persecuted
For righteousness' sake,
For theirs is the kingdom of heaven.
Blessed are you when they revile and persecute you,
And say all kinds of evil against you
falsely for My sake.
Rejoice and be exceedingly glad,
For great is your reward in heaven,
For so they persecuted the prophets
who were before you.

Matthew 5:3-4, 10-12

For I know the thoughts that I think toward
you, says the Lord, thoughts of peace and not
of evil, to give you a future and a hope.

Jeremiah 29:11

Emotions

Therefore, having been justified by faith,
We have peace with God through
our Lord Jesus Christ,
Through whom also we have access by faith
Into this grace in which we stand,
And rejoice in hope of the glory of God.
And not only that, but we also glory in tribulations,
Knowing that tribulation produces perseverance;
And perseverance, character; and character, hope.
Now hope does not disappoint,
Because the love of God has been
poured out in our hearts
By the Holy Spirit who was given to us.

Romans 5:1-5

Direction

When you have lost your way

Teaching them to observe all things that I have
commanded you; and lo,
I am with you always, even to the
end of the age. Amen.

Matthew 28:20

It is God who arms me with strength,
And makes my way perfect.

Psalm 18:32

Your word is a lamp to my feet
And a light to my path.

Psalm 119:105

A man's heart plans his way,
But the Lord directs his steps.

Proverbs 16:9

Stand fast therefore in the liberty
By which Christ has made us free,
And do not be entangled again
with a yoke of bondage.
Indeed I, Paul, say to you that if
you become circumcised,
Christ will profit you nothing.
And I testify again to every man
who becomes circumcised
That he is a debtor to keep the whole law.
You have become estranged from Christ,
You who attempt to be justified by law;
You have fallen from grace.
For we through the Spirit eagerly wait
for the Hope of righteousness by faith.
For in Christ Jesus neither circumcision
nor uncircumcision
Avails anything, but faith working through love.
You ran well. Who hindered you
from obeying the truth?

Galatians 5:1-7

Direction

When the future looks bleak

The steps of a good man are ordered by the Lord,
And He delights in his way.
Though he fall, he shall not be utterly cast down;
For the Lord upholds him with His hand.

Psalm 37:23-24

For I know the thoughts that I think toward you,
Says the Lord, thoughts of peace and not of evil,
To give you a future and a hope.

Jeremiah 29:11

For as the rain comes down,
and the snow from heaven,
And do not return there,
But water the earth,
And make it bring forth and bud,
That it may give seed to the sower
And bread to the eater,
So shall My word be that goes forth from My mouth;
It shall not return to Me void,
But it shall accomplish what I please,
And it shall prosper in the thing for which I sent it.

Isaiah 55:10-11

For He Himself has said, "I will never
leave you nor forsake you."

Hebrews 13:5b

When you need courage

Only be strong and very courageous,
That you may observe to do according to all the law
Which Moses My servant commanded you;
Do not turn from it to the right hand or to the left,
That you may prosper wherever you go.
This Book of the Law shall
not depart from your mouth,
But you shall meditate in it day and night,
That you may observe to do according to all
that is written in it.
For then you will make your way prosperous,
And then you will have good success.
Have I not commanded you?
Be strong and of good courage;
Do not be afraid, nor be dismayed,
For the Lord your God is with you wherever you go.

Joshua 1:7-9

The Lord is my light and my salvation;
Whom shall I fear?
The Lord is the strength of my life;
Of whom shall I be afraid?
When the wicked came against me
To eat up my flesh,
My enemies and foes,
They stumbled and fell.
Though an army may encamp against me,
My heart shall not fear;
Though war may rise against me,
In this I will be confident.

Psalm 27:1-3

Be of good courage,
And He shall strengthen your heart,
All you who hope in the Lord.

Psalm 31:24

For the Lord will be your confidence,
And will keep your foot from being caught.

Proverbs 3:26

In the fear of the Lord there is strong confidence,
And His children will have a place of refuge.

Proverbs 14:26

And the Philistine said to David,
"Come to me, and I will give your flesh
To the birds of the air
And the beasts of the field!"
Then David said to the Philistine,
"You come to me with a sword,
With a spear, and with a javelin.
But I come to you in the
Name of the Lord of hosts,
The God of the armies of Israel,
Whom you have defied.
This day the Lord will deliver you into my hand,
and I will strike you and take your head from you.
And this day I will give the carcasses
Of the camp of the Philistines to the birds of the air
And the wild beasts of the earth,
that all the earth may know that there is
a God in Israel.
Then all this assembly shall know that the Lord
Does not save with sword and spear;
For the battle is the Lord's, and He
will give you into our hands."

1 Samuel 17:44-47

Direction

I sought the Lord, and He heard me,
And delivered me from all my fears.
They looked to Him and were radiant,
And their faces were not ashamed.
This poor man cried out, and the Lord heard him,
And saved him out of all his troubles.
The angel of the Lord encamps all
around those who fear Him,
And delivers them.

Psalm 34:4-7

Who shall separate us from the love of Christ?
Shall tribulation, or distress, or persecution,
Or famine, or nakedness, or peril, or sword?
As it is written:
"For Your sake we are killed all day long;
We are accounted as sheep for the slaughter.
Yet in all these things we are more than
Conquerors through Him who loved us.

Romans 8:35-37

Shadrach, Meshach, and Abed-Nego
answered and said to the king,

"O Nebuchadnezzar, we have no need
to answer you in this matter.
If that is the case, our God whom we serve is
able to deliver us from the burning fiery furnace,
and He will deliver us from your hand, O king.
But if not, let it be known to you, O king, that
we do not serve your gods, nor will we worship
the gold image which you have set up."

Daniel 3:16-18

Though the fig tree may not blossom,
Nor fruit be on the vines;
Though the labor of the olive may fail,
And the fields yield no food;
Though the flock may be cut off from the fold,
And there be no herd in the stalls—
Yet I will rejoice in the Lord,
I will joy in the God of my salvation.
The Lord God is my strength;
He will make my feet like deer's feet,
And He will make me walk on my high hills.

Habakkuk 3:17-19

Direction

At my first defense no one stood with me,
But all forsook me. May it not be charged
against them.
But the Lord stood with me and strengthened me,
So that the message might be preached
fully through me,
And that all the Gentiles might hear.
Also I was delivered out of the mouth of the lion
And the Lord will deliver me from every evil work
And preserve me for His heavenly kingdom.
To Him be glory forever and ever. Amen!

2 Timothy 4:16-18

When seeking God's will

If anyone wills to do His will, He shall know
concerning the doctrine, whether it is from God
or whether I speak on My own authority.

John 7:17

You will show me the path of life;
In Your presence is fullness of joy;
At Your right hand are pleasures forevermore.

Psalm 16:11

The fear of the Lord is clean, enduring forever;
The judgments of the Lord are true
and righteous altogether.
More to be desired are they than gold,
Yea, than much fine gold;
Sweeter also than honey and the honeycomb.
Moreover by them Your servant is warned,
And in keeping them there is great reward.

Psalm 19:9-11

The Lord will perfect that which concerns me;
Your mercy, O Lord, endures forever;
Do not forsake the works of Your hands.

Psalm 138:8

I beseech you therefore, brethren, by the mercies
of God, that you present your bodies a living
sacrifice, holy, acceptable to God, which is your
reasonable service. And do not be conformed to
this world, but be transformed by the renewing
of your mind, that you may prove what is that
good and acceptable and perfect will of God.

Romans 12:1-2

Direction

Wait on the Lord,
And keep His way,
And He shall exalt you to inherit the land;
When the wicked are cut off, you shall see it.

Psalm 37:34

I say then: Walk in the Spirit,
And you shall not fulfill the lust of the flesh.
For the flesh lusts against the Spirit,
And the Spirit against the flesh;
And these are contrary to one another,
So that you do not do the things that you wish.

Galatians 5:16-17

When you need guidance

Trust in the Lord with all your heart,
And lean not on your own understanding;
In all your ways acknowledge Him,
And He shall direct your paths.

Proverbs 3:5-6

I will instruct you and teach you
In the way you should go;
I will guide you with My eye.

Psalm 32:8

However, when He, the Spirit of truth, has come,
He will guide you into all truth;
For He will not speak on His own authority,
But whatever He hears He will speak;
And He will tell you things to come.

John 16:13

All the paths of the Lord are mercy and truth,
To such as keep His covenant and His testimonies.

Psalm 25:10

Your word is a lamp to my feet
And a light to my path.

Psalm 119:105

The fear of the Lord is the beginning of wisdom;
A good understanding have all those
who do His commandments.
His praise endures forever.

Psalm 111:10

Direction

When you need direction

You in Your mercy have led forth
The people whom You have redeemed;
You have guided them in Your strength
To Your holy habitation.

Exodus 15:13

O Lord, You are the portion of my
inheritance and my cup;
You maintain my lot.
The lines have fallen to me in pleasant places;
Yes, I have a good inheritance.

Psalm 16:5-6

Then Moses said to the Lord, "See, You say to me
'Bring up this people,' But You have not let me know
whom You will send with me. Yet You have said,
"I know you by name, and you have also found
grace in My sight."
"Now therefore, I pray, if I have found grace in Your
sight, show me now Your way, that I may find grace
in Your sight" ... And He said, "My Presence will go
with you, and I will give you rest."

Exodus 34:13-14

Trust in Him at all times, you people;
Pour out your heart before Him;
God is a refuge for us.

Psalm 61:8

As for me, I will call upon God,
And the Lord shall save me.
Evening and morning and at noon
I will pray, and cry aloud,
And He shall hear my voice.

Psalm 55:16-17

Come and hear, all you who fear God,
And I will declare what He has done for my soul.
I cried to Him with my mouth,
And He was extolled with my tongue.
If I regard iniquity in my heart,
The Lord will not hear.
But certainly God has heard me;
He has attended to the voice of my prayer.
Blessed be God,
Who has not turned away my prayer,
Nor His mercy from me!

Psalm 66:16-20

Direction

So teach us to number our days,
That we may gain a heart of wisdom.

Psalm 90:12

Because You have been my help,
Therefore in the shadow of Your wings I will rejoice.
My soul follows close behind You;
Your right hand upholds me.

Psalm 63:7-8

When you seek wisdom

My son, pay attention to my wisdom;
Lend your ear to my understanding,
That you may preserve discretion,
And your lips may keep knowledge.

Proverbs 5:1-2

For the Lord gives wisdom;
From His mouth come knowledge and understanding;
He stores up sound wisdom for the upright;
He is a shield to those who walk uprightly.

Proverbs 2:6-7

Wisdom is good with an inheritance,
And profitable to those who see the sun.
For wisdom is a defense as money is a defense,
But the excellence of knowledge is that
wisdom gives life to those who have it.

Ecclesiastes 7:11-12

Wisdom is better than weapons of war...

Ecclesiastes 9:18a

Who is wise and understanding among you?
Let him show by good conduct that his works
Are done in the meekness of wisdom.
But if you have bitter envy and
self-seeking in your hearts,
Do not boast and lie against the truth.
This wisdom does not descend from above,
But is earthly, sensual, demonic.
For where envy and self-seeking exist,
Confusion and every evil thing are there.
But the wisdom that is from above is first pure,
Then peaceable, gentle, willing to yield,
Full of mercy and good fruits,
Without partiality and without hypocrisy.

James 3:13-17

Direction

Yes, if you cry out for discernment,
And lift up your voice for understanding,
If you seek her as silver,
And search for her as for hidden treasures;
Then you will understand the fear of the Lord,
And find the knowledge of God.

Proverbs 2:3-5

Get Wisdom! Get understanding!
Do not forget, nor turn away
from the words of my mouth.
Do not forsake her, and she will preserve you;
Love her, and she will keep you.
Wisdom is the principal thing;
Therefore get wisdom.
And in all your getting, get understanding.

Proverbs 4:5-7

If any of you lacks wisdom, let him ask of God,
Who gives to all liberally and without reproach,
And it will be given to him.

James 1:5

Let the word of Christ
dwell in you richly in all wisdom,
Teaching and admonishing one another in psalms
And hymns and spiritual songs,
Singing with grace in your hearts to the Lord.

Colossians 3:16

See then that you walk circumspectly,
Not as fools but as wise, redeeming the time,
Because the days are evil.

Ephesians 5:15-16

Happy is the man who finds wisdom,
And the man who gains understanding;
For her proceeds are better than the profits of silver,
And her gain than fine gold.
She is more precious than rubies,
And all the things you may desire
cannot compare with her.
Length of days is in her right hand,
In her left hand riches and honor.
Her ways are ways of pleasantness,
And all her paths are peace.
She is a tree of life to those who take hold of her,
And happy are all who retain her.

Proverbs 3:13-18

Direction

Then Jesus spoke to them again, saying,
"I am the light of the world.
He who follows Me shall not walk in darkness,
But have the light of life."

John 8:12

Great is our Lord,
and mighty in power;
His understanding is infinite.

Psalm 147:5

Let no one deceive himself.
If anyone among you seems to be wise in this age,
Let him become a fool that he may become wise.
For the wisdom of this world is foolishness with God.
For it is written,
"He catches the wise in their own craftiness";
And again,
"The Lord knows the thoughts of
the wise, that they are futile."

1 Corinthians 3:18-20

A man who isolates himself seeks his own desire;
He rages against all wise judgment.

Proverbs 18:1

When wisdom enters your heart
And knowledge is pleasant to your soul,
Discretion will preserve you;
Understanding will keep you.

Proverbs 2:10-11

When self-discipline escapes you

Be diligent to present yourself approved to God,
A worker who does not need to be ashamed,
Rightly dividing the word of truth.

2 Timothy 2:15

But be doers of the word, and not hearers only,
deceiving yourselves. For if anyone is a hearer
of the word and not a doer, he is like a man
observing his natural face in a mirror; for he
observes himself, goes away, and immediately
forgets what kind of man he was. But he who looks
into the perfect law of liberty and continues in
it, and is not a forgetful hearer but a doer of the
work, this one will be blessed in what he does.

If anyone among you thinks he is religious, and does not bridle his tongue but deceives his own heart, this one's religion is useless. Pure and undefiled religion before God and the Father is this: to visit orphans and widows in their trouble, and to keep oneself unspotted from the world.

James 1:22-27

Set your mind on things above,
not on things on the earth.

Colossians 3:2

But the fruit of the Spirit is love, joy, peace,
Longsuffering, kindness, goodness, faithfulness,
Gentleness, self-control. Against such there is no law.

Galatians 5:22-23

Finally, brethren, whatever things are true, whatever things are noble, whatever things are just, whatever things are pure, whatever things are lovely, whatever things are of good report, if there is any virtue and if there is anything praiseworthy— meditate on these things. The things which you learned and received and heard and saw in me, these do, and the God of peace will be with you.

Philippians 4:8-9

Do you not know that those who run in a race all run,
But one receives the prize?
Run in such a way that you may obtain it.
And everyone who competes for the prize
Is temperate in all things.
Now they do it to obtain a perishable crown,
But we for an imperishable crown.
Therefore I run thus: not with uncertainty.
Thus I fight: not as one who beats the air.
But I discipline my body and bring it into subjection,
Lest, when I have preached to others,
I myself should become disqualified.

                                    1 Corinthians 9:24-27

Come now, you who say, "Today or tomorrow we
will go to such and such a city, spend a
year there, buy and sell, and make a profit"; whereas
you do not know what will happen
tomorrow. For what is your life? It is even a vapor
that appears for a little time and then vanishes
away. Instead you ought to say, "If the Lord
wills, we shall live and do this or that."

                                    James 4:13-15

Direction

SET YOUR MIND

ON THINGS ABOVE,

NOT ON THINGS

ON THE EARTH.

COLOSSIANS 3:2

Christian
Life

When you want to accept Jesus as Savior

If you confess with your mouth the Lord Jesus
And believe in your heart that God has raised
Him from the dead, you will be saved.

Romans 10:9

For God so loved the world
That He gave His only begotten Son,
That whoever believes in Him
Should not perish but have everlasting life.

John 3:16

Whoever believes that Jesus is the
Christ is born of God,
And everyone who loves Him
who begot also loves him
who is begotten of Him...
These things I have written to you who believe
In the name of the Son of God,
That you may know that you have eternal life,
And that you may continue to believe
In the name of the Son of God.

1 John 5:1, 13

But God demonstrates His own love toward us,
In that while we were still sinners,
Christ died for us.

Romans 5:8

Jesus said to him, "I am the way, the truth, and the
life. No one comes to the Father except through Me."

John 14:6

And she will bring forth a Son, and you
shall call His name Jesus, for He will
save His people from their sins.

Matthew 1:21

There is therefore now no condemnation to
those who are in Christ Jesus, who do not walk
according to the flesh, but walk according to
the Spirit. For the law of the Spirit of life has
made me free from the law of sin and death.

Romans 8:1-2

For "whoever calls on the name of
the Lord shall be saved."

Romans 10:13

Christian Life

When sin needs to be confessed

I acknowledged my sin to You,
And my iniquity I have not hidden.
I said, "I will confess my transgressions to the Lord,"
And You forgave the iniquity of my sin.

Psalm 32:5

He who covers his sins will not prosper,
But whoever confesses and forsakes
Them will have mercy.

Proverbs 28:13

If we confess our sins,
He is faithful and just to forgive us our sins
And to cleanse us from all unrighteousness.

1 John 1:9

Create in me a clean heart, O God,
And renew a steadfast spirit within me.
Do not cast me away from Your presence,
And do not take Your Holy Spirit from me.
Restore to me the joy of Your salvation,
And uphold me by Your generous Spirit.

Psalm 51:10-12

Let the wicked forsake his way,
And the unrighteous man his thoughts;
Let him return to the Lord,
And He will have mercy on him;
And to our God,
For He will abundantly pardon.

Isaiah 55:7

Behold, the Lord's hand is not shortened,
That it cannot save;
Nor His ear heavy,
That it cannot hear.
But your iniquities have separated
you from your God;
And your sins have hidden His face from you,
So that He will not hear.

Isaiah 59:1-2

He who conceals his sin does not prosper, but
whoever confesses and renounces them finds mercy.

Proverbs 28:13

Christian Life

When you need grace

For the grace of God that brings salvation has
appeared to all men, teaching us that, denying
ungodliness and worldly lusts, we should live
soberly, righteously, and godly in the present age,
looking for the blessed hope and glorious appearing
of our great God and Savior Jesus Christ, who
gave Himself for us, that He might redeem us
from every lawless deed and purify for Himself
His own special people, zealous for good works.

Titus 2:11-14

But He gives more grace.
Therefore He says:
"God resists the proud,
But gives grace to the humble."

James 4:6

And the grace of our Lord was exceedingly abundant,
with faith and love which are in Christ Jesus.

1 Timothy 1:12-17

Therefore do not let sin reign in your mortal body,
That you should obey it in its lusts.
And do not present your members
As instruments of unrighteousness to sin,
But present yourselves to God
As being alive from the dead,
And your members as instruments
of righteousness to God.
For sin shall not have dominion over you,
For you are not under law but under grace.

Romans 6:12-14

For there is no difference; for all have sinned and
fall short of the glory of God, being justified freely
by His grace through the redemption that is in
Christ Jesus, whom God set forth as a propitiation
by His blood, through faith, to demonstrate His
righteousness, because in His forbearance God
had passed over the sins that were previously
committed, to demonstrate at the present time
His righteousness, that He might be just and
the justifier of the one who has faith in Jesus.

Romans 3:22b-26

Christian Life

And he arose and came to his father. But when he was still a great way off, his father saw him and had compassion, and ran and fell on his neck and kissed him. And the son said to him, "Father, I have sinned against heaven and in your sight, and am no longer worthy to be called your son."

But the father said to his servants, "Bring out the best robe and put it on him, and put a ring on his hand and sandals on his feet. And bring the fatted calf here and kill it, and let us eat and be merry; for this my son was dead and is alive again; he was lost and is found." And they began to be merry.

Luke 15:20-24

Everyone who believes in him [Jesus] receives forgiveness of sin through His name.

Acts 10:43

When you need God's mercy

Who is a God like You,
Pardoning iniquity
And passing over the transgression of the remnant of
His heritage?
He does not retain His anger forever,
Because He delights in mercy.

Micah 7:18

Through the Lord's mercies we are not consumed,
Because His compassions fail not.
They are new every morning;
Great is Your faithfulness.
"The Lord is my portion," says my soul,
"Therefore I hope in Him!"

Lamentations 3:22-24

Cast your burden on the Lord,
And He shall sustain you;
He shall never permit the righteous to be moved.

Psalm 55:22

This is a faithful saying and worthy of all
acceptance, that Christ Jesus came into the world
to save sinners, of whom I am chief. However,
for this reason I obtained mercy, that in me first
Jesus Christ might show all longsuffering, as a
pattern to those who are going to believe on Him
for everlasting life. Now to the King eternal,
immortal, invisible, to God who alone is wise,
be honor and glory forever and ever. Amen.

1 Timothy 1:15-17

Blessed are the merciful,
For they shall obtain mercy.

Matthew 5:7

So speak and so do as those who
Will be judged by the law of liberty.
For judgment is without mercy
To the one who has shown no mercy.
Mercy triumphs over judgment.

James 2:12-13

With the merciful You will show Yourself merciful;
With a blameless man You will
show Yourself blameless.

2 Samuel 22:26

When you feel spiritually unworthy

Jesus answered and said to them, "Those who are well have no need of a physician, but those who are sick. I have not come to call the righteous, but sinners, to repentance."

Luke 5:31-32

...being confident of this very thing, that He who has begun a good work in you will complete it until the day of Jesus Christ.

Philippians 1:6

As it is written:
"There is none righteous, no, not one;
There is none who understands;
There is none who seeks after God.
They have all turned aside;
They have together become unprofitable;
There is none who does good, no, not one."

Romans 3:10-12

For all have sinned and fall short of the glory of God, being justified freely by His grace through the redemption that is in Christ Jesus, whom God set forth as a propitiation by His blood, through

Christian Life

faith, to demonstrate His righteousness, because in His forbearance God had passed over the sins that were previously committed, to demonstrate at the present time His righteousness, that He might be just and the justifier of the one who has faith in Jesus.

Romans 3:23-26

Blessed are the poor in spirit,
For theirs is the kingdom of heaven.
Blessed are those who mourn,
For they shall be comforted.
Blessed are the meek,
For they shall inherit the earth.
Blessed are those who hunger and
thirst for righteousness,
For they shall be filled.
Blessed are the merciful,
For they shall obtain mercy.
Blessed are the pure in heart,
For they shall see God.
Blessed are the peacemakers,
For they shall be called sons of God.
Blessed are those who are persecuted for
righteousness' sake,
For theirs is the kingdom of heaven.

Matthew 5:3-10

For by grace you have been saved through
faith, and that not of yourselves; it is the gift of
God, not of works, lest anyone should boast.

Ephesians 2:8-9

This is a faithful saying and worthy of all acceptance,
That Christ Jesus came into the world to save sinners,
Of whom I am chief.
However, for this reason I obtained mercy,
That in me first Jesus Christ
might show all longsuffering,
As a pattern to those who are going to
believe on Him for everlasting life.

1 Timothy 1:15-16

The name of the Lord is a strong tower;
The righteous run to it and are safe.

Proverbs 18:10

Fear not, for I am with you;
Be not dismayed, for I am your God.
I will strengthen you,
Yes, I will help you,
I will uphold you with My righteous right hand.

Isaiah 41:10

Christian Life

Have you not known?
Have you not heard?
The everlasting God, the Lord,
The Creator of the ends of the earth,
Neither faints nor is weary.
His understanding is unsearchable.
He gives power to the weak,
And to those who have no might
He increases strength.
Even the youths shall faint and be weary,
And the young men shall utterly fall,
But those who wait on the Lord
Shall renew their strength;
They shall mount up with wings like eagles,
They shall run and not be weary,
They shall walk and not faint.

Isaiah 40:28-31

When you feel unloved

But God demonstrates His own love toward us, in
that while we were still sinners, Christ died for us.

Romans 5:8

Now before the Feast of the Passover, when Jesus
knew that His hour had come that He should depart
from this world to the Father, having loved His own
who were in the world, He loved them to the end.

John 13:1

And He Himself is the propitiation for our sins, and
not for ours only but also for the whole world.

1 John 2:2

You have hedged me behind and before,
And laid Your hand upon me.
Such knowledge is too wonderful for me;
It is high, I cannot attain it.

Psalm 139:5-6

For You formed my inward parts;
You covered me in my mother's womb.
I will praise You, for I am fearfully
and wonderfully made;
Marvelous are Your works,
And that my soul knows very well.
My frame was not hidden from You,
When I was made in secret,
And skillfully wrought in the
lowest parts of the earth.
Your eyes saw my substance, being yet unformed.
And in Your book they all were written,
The days fashioned for me,
When as yet there were none of them.

Psalm 139:13-16

For I am persuaded that neither death nor life,
Nor angels nor principalities nor powers,
Or things present nor things to come,
nor height nor depth,
Nor any other created thing,
Shall be able to separate us from the love of God
Which is in Christ Jesus our Lord.

Romans 8:38-39

See to it that no one misses the grace of
God and that no bitter root grows up
to cause trouble and defile many.

Hebrews 12:15

The Lord has appeared of old to me, saying:
"Yes, I have loved you with an everlasting love;
Therefore with lovingkindness I have drawn you.

Jeremiah 31:3

Through the Lord's mercies we are not consumed,
Because His compassions fail not.
They are new every morning;
Great is Your faithfulness.

Lamentations 3:22-23

When you think your prayers have not been answered

Now this is the confidence that we have in Him,
That if we ask anything according to His will,
He hears us. And if we know that He hears us,
Whatever we ask, we know that we have
The petitions that we have asked of Him.

1 John 5:14-15

Christian Life

Then you will call upon Me and go and pray to Me,
And I will listen to you.
And you will seek Me and find Me,
When you search for Me with all your heart.

Jeremiah 29:12-13

Yet you do not have because you do not ask.
You ask and do not receive,
Because you ask amiss,
That you may spend it on your pleasures.

James 4:2b-3

Be anxious for nothing,
But in everything by prayer and supplication,
With thanksgiving, let your requests
be made known to God,
And the peace of God which surpasses
all understanding,
Will guard your hearts and minds
through Christ Jesus.

Philippians 4:6-7

If I regard iniquity in my heart,
the Lord will not hear.
But certainly God has heard me;
He has attended to the voice of my prayer.

Psalm 66:18-19

O LORD, God of my salvation,
I have cried out day and night before You.
Let my prayer come before You;
Incline Your ear to my cry.
The LORD is near to all who call upon Him,
To all who call upon Him in truth.

Psalm 145:18

If any of you lacks wisdom, let him ask of God,
Who gives liberally and without reproach,
And it will be given to him.
But let him ask in faith, with no doubting,
For he who doubts is like a wave of the sea
Driven and tossed by the wind.
For let not that man suppose that he will receive
Anything from the Lord;
He is a double-minded man, unstable in all his ways.

James 1:5-8

But I say to you, love your enemies,
Bless those who curse you,
Do good to those who hate you,
And pray for those who spitefully
Use you and persecute you.

Matthew 5:44

Christian Life

Elijah was a man with a nature like ours,
And he prayed earnestly that it would not rain;
And it did not rain on the land
for three years and six months.
And he prayed again, and the heaven gave rain,
And the earth produced its fruit.

James 5:17-18

The righteous cry out, and the LORD hears,
And delivers them out of all their troubles.
The LORD is near to those who have a broken heart,
And saves such as have a contrite spirit.

Psalm 34:-17-18

Let us come boldly to the throne of grace,
That we may obtain mercy and find grace
To help in the time of need.

Hebrews 4:16

Confess your trespasses to one another,
And pray for one another,
That you may be healed.
The effective, fervent prayer of a
righteous man avails much.

James 5:16

Again I say to you that if two of you agree on earth
concerning anything that they ask,
It will be done for them by My Father in heaven.
For where two or three are gathered
together in My name,
I am there in the midst of them.

Matthew 18:19-20

Trust in the Lord, and do good;
Dwell in the land, and feed on His faithfulness.
Delight yourself also in the Lord,
And He shall give you the desires of your heart.
Commit your way to the Lord,
Trust also in Him,
And He shall bring it to pass.
He shall bring forth your righteousness as the light,
And your justice as the noonday.
Rest in the Lord, and wait patiently for Him;
Do not fret because of him who prospers in his way,
Because of the man who brings
wicked schemes to pass.

Psalm 37:3-7

Christian Life

When you need strength

The Lord is near to all who call upon Him,
To all who call upon Him in truth.

Psalm 145:18

Is anyone among you suffering?
Let him pray.
Is anyone cheerful?
Let him sing psalms.
Is anyone among you sick?
Let him call for the elders of the church,
And let them pray over him,
Anointing him with oil in the name of the Lord.
And the prayer of faith will save the sick,
And the Lord will raise him up.

James 5:13-15

The Lord is my strength and song,
And He has become my salvation;
He is my God, and I will praise Him;
My father's God, and I will exalt Him.

Exodus 15:2

Hear my cry, O God;
Attend to my prayer.
From the end of the earth I will cry to You,
When my heart is overwhelmed;
Lead me to the rock that is higher than I.
For You have been a shelter for me,
A strong tower from the enemy.
I will abide in Your tabernacle forever;
I will trust in the shelter of Your wings.

Psalm 61:1-4

Seek the Lord and His strength;
Seek His face evermore!

1 Chronicles 16:11

I can do all things through Christ
who strengthens me.

Philippians 4:13

Now David was greatly distressed,
For the people spoke of stoning him,
Because the soul of all the people was grieved,
Every man for his sons and his daughters.
But David strengthened himself in the Lord his God.

1 Samuel 30:6

Christian Life

I will love You, O Lord, my strength.
The Lord is my rock and my fortress
and my deliverer;
My God, my strength, in whom I will trust;
My shield and the horn of my salvation,
my stronghold.
I will call upon the Lord, who is worthy to be praised;
So shall I be saved from my enemies ...
For who is God, except the Lord?
And who is a rock, except our God?
It is God who arms me with strength,
And makes my way perfect.
He makes my feet like the feet of deer,
And sets me on my high places.
He teaches my hands to make war,
So that my arms can bend a bow of bronze.

Psalm 18:1-3, 31-34

Have I not commanded you?
Be strong and of good courage;
Do not be afraid, nor be dismayed,
For the Lord your God is with you wherever you go.

Joshua 1:9

Concerning this thing I pleaded with the Lord
Three times that it might depart from me.
And He said to me, "My grace is sufficient for you,
For My strength is made perfect in weakness."
Therefore most gladly I will rather boast in my
infirmities, That the power of Christ may rest upon
me. Therefore I take pleasure in infirmities, in
reproaches, In needs, in persecutions, in distresses, for
Christ's sake. For when I am weak, then I am strong.

2 Corinthians 12:8-10

No temptation has overtaken you except such as
is common to man; but God is faithful, who will
not allow you to be tempted beyond what you are
able, but with the temptation will also make the
way of escape, that you may be able to bear it.

1 Corinthians 10:13

The Lord is my strength and song,
And He has become my salvation;
He is my God, and I will praise Him;
My father's God, and I will exalt Him.

Exodus 15:2

Christian Life

Have you not known?
Have you not heard?
The everlasting God, the Lord,
The Creator of the ends of the earth,
Neither faints nor is weary.
His understanding is unsearchable.
He gives power to the weak,
And to those who have no might
He increases strength.
Even the youths shall faint and be weary,
And the young men shall utterly fall,
But those who wait on the Lord
Shall renew their strength;
They shall mount up with wings like eagles,
They shall run and not be weary,
They shall walk and not faint.

Isaiah 40:28-31

The Lord is my light and my salvation;
Whom shall I fear?
The Lord is the strength of my life;
Of whom shall I be afraid?

Psalm 27:1

So Jesus said to them, "Because of your unbelief;
for assuredly, I say to you, if you have faith as
a mustard seed, you will say to this mountain,
'Move from here to there,' and it will move;
and nothing will be impossible for you."

Matthew 17:20

For God has not given us a spirit of fear, but
of power and of love and of a sound mind.

2 Timothy 1:7

When you've lost confidence

I charge you therefore before God and the Lord
Jesus Christ, who will judge the living and the dead
at His appearing and his Kingdom: Preach the word!
Be ready in season and out of season. Convince,
rebuke, exhort, with all longsuffering and teaching.

2 Timothy 4:1-2

Therefore do not cast away your confidence,
which has great reward. For you have need
of endurance, so that after you have done the
will of God, you may receive the promise.

Hebrews 10:35-36

Christian Life

And we know that all things work together
For good to those who love God,
To those who are the called
According to His purpose.

Romans 8:28

Blessed is the man who trusts in the Lord,
And whose hope is the Lord.
For he shall be like a tree planted by the waters,
Which spreads out its roots by the river,
And will not fear when heat comes;
But its leaf will be green,
And will not be anxious in the year of drought,
Nor will cease from yielding fruit.

Jeremiah 17:7-8

If then you were raised with Christ, seek those
things which are above, where Christ is, sitting
at the right hand of God. Set your mind on things
above, not on things on the earth. For you died, and
your life is hidden with Christ in God. When Christ
who is our life appears, then you also will appear with
Him in glory.

Colossians 3:1-4

And let us consider one another in order to stir up love and good works, not forsaking the assembling of ourselves together, as is the manner of some, but exhorting one another, and so much the more as you see the Day approaching.

Hebrews 10:24-25

When you need to speak truth

Sanctify them by Your truth. Your word is truth.

John 17:17

Then Jesus said to those Jews who believed Him, "If you abide in My word, you are My disciples indeed. And you shall know the truth, and the truth shall make you free."

John 8:31-32

Do not lie to one another, since you have put off the old man with his deeds and have put on the new man who is renewed in knowledge according to the image of Him who created Him.

Colossians 3:9-10

Christian Life

My little children, let us not love in word
or in tongue, but in deed and in truth.

1 John 3:18

"These are the things you shall do:
Speak each man the truth to his neighbor;
Give judgment in your gates for truth,
justice, and peace;
Let none of you think evil in your heart
against your neighbor;
And do not love a false oath.
For all these are things that I hate,"
Says the Lord.

Zechariah 8:16-17

Lord, who may abide in Your tabernacle?
Who may dwell in Your holy hill?
He who walks uprightly,
And works righteousness,
And speaks the truth in his heart;

Psalm 15:1-2

That we should no longer be children, tossed
to and fro and carried about with every wind of
doctrine, by the trickery of men, in the cunning
craftiness of deceitful plotting, but, speaking the
truth in love, may grow up in all things into Him
who is the head—Christ—from whom the whole
body, joined and knit together by what every joint
supplies, according to the effective working by
which every part does its share, causes growth
of the body for the edifying of itself in love.

Ephesians 4:14-16

A true witness delivers souls,
But a deceitful witness speaks lies.

Proverbs 14:25

Therefore, putting away lying,
Let each one of you speak truth with his neighbor,
For we are members of one another.

Ephesians 4:25

A false witness will not go unpunished,
And he who speaks lies will not escape.

Proverbs 19:5

Christian Life

When you need to forgive

For if you forgive men their trespasses, your heavenly Father will also forgive you.

Matthew 6:14

Keep justice and do righteousness. For my salvation is about to come, and my righteousness to be revealed. Blessed is the man who does this...

Isaiah 56:1-2a

And whenever you stand praying,
If you have anything against anyone,
Forgive him, that your Father in heaven
May also forgive you your trespasses.

Mark 11:25

Take heed to yourselves. If your brother sins against you, rebuke him; and if he repents, forgive him. And if he sins against you seven times in a day, and seven times in a day returns to you, saying, "I repent," you shall forgive him.

Luke 17:3-4

And be kind to one another, tenderhearted,
forgiving one another, even as
God in Christ forgave you.

Ephesians 4:32

Therefore, as the elect of God, holy and beloved,
Put on tender mercies, kindness, humility, meekness,
Longsuffering; bearing with one another,
And forgiving one another,
If anyone has a complaint against another;
Even as Christ forgave you, so you also must do.

Colossians 3:12-13

For all have sinned and fall short of the glory of God.

Romans 3:23

Bear with each other and forgive whatever
grievances you may have against one another.
Forgive as the Lord forgave you.

Colossians 3:13

Christian Life

When you need to ask forgiveness

Let the wicked forsake his way,
And the unrighteous man his thoughts;
Let him return to the Lord,
And He will have mercy on him;
And to our God,
For He will abundantly pardon.

Isaiah 55:7

Who is a God like You,
Pardoning iniquity
And passing over the transgression
of the remnant of His heritage?
He does not retain His anger forever,
Because He delights in mercy.
He will again have compassion on us,
And will subdue our iniquities.
You will cast all our sins
Into the depths of the sea.
You will give truth to Jacob
And mercy to Abraham,
Which You have sworn to our fathers
From days of old.

Micah 7:18-20

In Him we have redemption through
His blood, the forgiveness of sins,
according to the riches of His grace.

Ephesians 1:7

To the Lord our God *belong* mercy and forgiveness,
though we have rebelled against Him.

Daniel 9:9

For if you forgive men their trespasses, your
heavenly Father will also forgive you. But if
you do not forgive men their trespasses, neither
will your Father forgive your trespasses.

Matthew 6:14-15

Purge me with hyssop, and I shall be clean;
Wash me, and I shall be whiter than snow.
Make me hear joy and gladness,
That the bones You have broken may rejoice.
Hide Your face from my sins,
And blot out all my iniquities.
Create in me a clean heart, O God,
And renew a steadfast spirit within me.

Psalm 51:7-11

Christian Life

As far as the east is from the west,
So far has He removed our transgressions from us.

Psalm 103:12

If we confess our sins,
He is faithful and just to forgive us our sins
And to cleanse us from all unrighteousness.

1 John 1:9

When you need to love your enemy

But I say to you, love your enemies,
Bless those who curse you,
Do good to those who hate you,
And pray for those who spitefully
Use you and persecute you.

Matthew 5:44

He who says he is in the light, and hates his brother,
is in darkness until now. He who loves his brother
abides in the light, and there is no cause for stumbling
in him. But he who hates his brother is in darkness
and walks in darkness, and does not know where he
is going, because the darkness has blinded his eyes.

1 John 2:9-11

Let all bitterness, wrath, anger, clamor, and evil
speaking be put away from you, with all malice. And
be kind to one another, tenderhearted, forgiving
one another, even as God in Christ forgave you.

Ephesians 4:31-32

Repay no one evil for evil. Have regard
for good things in the sight of all men.

Romans 12:17

When you are weary in well-doing

And let us not grow weary while doing good,
For in due season we shall reap
if we do not lose heart.

Galatians 6:9

A merry heart does good, like medicine,
But a broken spirit dries the bones.

Proverbs 17:22

The desire of the lazy man kills him,
For his hands refuse to labor.
He covets greedily all day long,
But the righteous gives and does not spare.

Proverbs 21:25-26

Who "will render to each one according to
his deeds": eternal life to those who by patient
continuance in doing good seek for glory, honor,
and immortality; but to those who are self-
seeking and do not obey the truth, but obey
unrighteousness—indignation and wrath.

Romans 2:6-8

When you desire victory

The eternal God is your refuge,
And underneath are the everlasting arms;
He will thrust out the enemy from before you,
And will say, "Destroy!"

Deuteronomy 33:27

For by You I can run against a troop,
By my God I can leap over a wall.

Psalm 18:29

Some trust in chariots, and some in horses;
But we will remember the name of the Lord our God.
They have bowed down and fallen;
But we have risen and stand upright.

Psalm 20:7-8

The Lord upholds all who fall,
And raises up all who are bowed down.

Psalm 145:14

And not only that, but we also glory in tribulations,
Knowing that tribulation produces perseverance;
And perseverance, character; and character, hope.
Now hope does not disappoint,
Because the love of God has been
poured out in our hearts
By the Holy Spirit who was given to us.

Romans 5:3-5

Being confident of this very thing,
that He who has begun a good work in you will
complete it until the day of Jesus Christ.

Philippians 1:6

Christian Life

He gives power to the weak,
And to those who have no might
He increases strength.
Even the youths shall faint and be weary,
And the young men shall utterly fall,
But those who wait on the Lord
Shall renew their strength;
They shall mount up with wings like eagles,
They shall run and not be weary,
They shall walk and not faint.

Isaiah 40:29-31

So when this corruptible has put on incorruption,
And this mortal has put on immortality,
Then shall be brought to pass
the saying that is written:
"Death is swallowed up in victory."
"O Death, where is your sting?
O Hades, where is your victory?"
The sting of death is sin,
And the strength of sin is the law.
But thanks be to God, who gives us the victory
Through our Lord Jesus Christ.

1 Corinthians 15:54-57

And we have such trust through Christ toward God.
Not that we are sufficient of ourselves to think of
anything as being from ourselves, but our sufficiency
is from God, who also made us sufficient as ministers
of the new covenant, not of the letter but of the
Spirit; for the letter kills, but the Spirit gives life.

2 Corinthians 3:4-6

When I cry out to You,
Then my enemies will turn back;
This I know, because God is for me.

Psalm 56:9

And now, little children, abide in Him, that when
He appears, we may have confidence and not be
ashamed before Him at His coming. If you know
that He is righteous, you know that everyone
who practices righteousness is born of Him.

1 John 2:28-29

Christian Life

When you have been disobedient

Search me, O God, and know my heart;
Try me, and know my anxieties;
And see if there is any wicked way in me,
And lead me in the way everlasting.

Psalm 139:23-24

The Lord is near to all who call upon Him,
To all who call upon Him in truth.

Psalm 145:18

Now I rejoice, not that you were made sorry,
but that your sorrow led to repentance. For you
were made sorry in a godly manner, that you
might suffer loss from us in nothing. For godly
sorrow produces repentance leading to salvation,
not to be regretted; but the sorrow of the world
produces death. For observe this very thing, that
you sorrowed in a godly manner: What diligence
it produced in you, what clearing of yourselves,
what indignation, what fear, what vehement
desire, what zeal, what vindication! In all things
you proved yourselves to be clear in this matter.

2 Corinthians 7:9-11

And you have forgotten the exhortation
which speaks to you as to sons:
"My son, do not despise the chastening of the Lord,
Nor be discouraged when you are rebuked by Him;
For whom the Lord loves He chastens,
And scourges every son whom He receives."
If you endure chastening, God deals with you as
with sons; for what son is there whom a father does
not chasten? But if you are without chastening,
of which all have become partakers, then you are
illegitimate and not sons. Furthermore, we have
had human fathers who corrected us, and we paid
them respect. Shall we not much more readily be
in subjection to the Father of spirits and live? For
they indeed for a few days chastened us as seemed
best to them, but He for our profit, that we may
be partakers of His holiness. Now no chastening
seems to be joyful for the present, but painful;
nevertheless, afterward it yields the peaceable fruit of
righteousness to those who have been trained by it.

Hebrews 12:5-11

Christian Life

When you are tempted to judge

Judge not, that you be not judged. For with what judgment you judge, you will be judged; and with the measure you use, it will be measured back to you. And why do you look at the speck in your brother's eye, but do not consider the plank in your own eye? Or how can you say to your brother, "Let me remove the speck from your eye;" and look, a plank is in your own eye? Hypocrite! First remove the plank from your own eye, and then you will see clearly to remove the speck from your brother's eye.

Matthew 7:1-5

Open your mouth, judge righteously,
And plead the cause of the poor and needy.

Proverbs 31:9

Do not speak evil of one another, brethren. He who speaks evil of a brother and judges his brother, speaks evil of the law and judges the law. But if you judge the law, you are not a doer of the law but a judge. There is one Lawgiver, who is able to save and to destroy. Who are you to judge another?

James 4:11-12

Let no corrupt word proceed out of your mouth,
but what is good for necessary edification,
that it may impart grace to the hearers.

Ephesians 4:29

For all the law is fulfilled in one word, even in this:
"You shall love your neighbor as yourself."

Galatians 5:14

Remind them ... speak evil of no one, to be
peaceable, gentle, showing all humility to all men.
For we ourselves were also once foolish, disobedient,
deceived, serving various lusts and pleasures, living
in malice and envy, hateful and hating one another.
But when the kindness and the love of God our Savior
toward man appeared, not by works of righteousness
which we have done, but according to His mercy He
saved us, through the washing of regeneration and
renewing of the Holy Spirit, whom He poured out
on us abundantly through Jesus Christ our Savior,
that having been justified by His grace we should
become heirs according to the hope of eternal life.

Titus 3:1-7

Christian Life

Therefore you are inexcusable, O man, whoever you
are who judge, for in whatever you judge another
you condemn yourself; for you who judge practice
the same things. But we know that the judgment of
God is according to truth against those who practice
such things. And do you think this, O man, you who
judge those practicing such things, and doing the
same, that you will escape the judgment of God?

Romans 2:1-3

Brethren, if a man is overtaken in any trespass,
you who are spiritual restore such a one in a spirit
of gentleness, considering yourself lest you also
be tempted. Bear one another's burdens, and
so fulfill the law of Christ. For if anyone thinks
himself to be something, when he is nothing, he
deceives himself. But let each one examine his own
work, and then he will have rejoicing in himself
alone, and not in another. For each one shall bear
his own load. Let him who is taught the word
share in all good things with him who teaches.

Galatians 6:1-6

And above all things have fervent love for one
another, for "love will cover a multitude of sins."
Be hospitable to one another without grumbling.

1 Peter 4:8-9

Two men went up to the temple to pray, one a
Pharisee and the other a tax collector. The Pharisee
stood and prayed thus with himself, "God, I thank
You that I am not like other men—extortioners,
unjust, adulterers, or even as this tax collector. I fast
twice a week; I give tithes of all that I possess." And
the tax collector, standing afar off, would not so much
as raise his eyes to heaven, but beat his breast, saying,
"God, be merciful to me a sinner!" I tell you, this man
went down to his house justified rather than the other;
for everyone who exalts himself will be humbled,
and he who humbles himself will be exalted.

Luke 18:10-14

Christian Life

When your tongue is getting you in trouble

Even so the tongue is a little member and boasts great things. See how great a forest a little fire kindles! And the tongue is a fire, a world of iniquity. The tongue is so set among our members that it defiles the whole body, and sets on fire the course of nature; and it is set on fire by hell. For every kind of beast and bird, of reptile and creature of the sea, is tamed and has been tamed by mankind. But no man can tame the tongue. It is an unruly evil, full of deadly poison. With it we bless our God and Father, and with it we curse men, who have been made in the similitude of God. Out of the same mouth proceed blessing and cursing. My brethren, these things ought not to be so. Does a spring send forth fresh water and bitter from the same opening? Can a fig tree, my brethren, bear olives, or a grapevine bear figs? Thus no spring yields both salt water and fresh.

James 3:5-12

In the multitude of words sin is not lacking,
But he who restrains his lips is wise.

Proverbs 10:19

If anyone among you thinks he is religious,
and does not bridle his tongue but deceives his
own heart, this one's religion is useless.

James 1:26

But I say to you that for every idle word men may
speak, they will give account of it in the day of
judgment. For by your words you will be justified,
and by your words you will be condemned.

Matthew 12:36-37

These six things the Lord hates,
Yes, seven are an abomination to Him:
A proud look,
A lying tongue,
Hands that shed innocent blood,
A heart that devises wicked plans,
Feet that are swift in running to evil,
A false witness who speaks lies,
And one who sows discord among brethren.

Proverbs 6:16-19

Let no corrupt word proceed out of your mouth,
but what is good for necessary edification,
that it may impart grace to the hearers.

Ephesians 4:29

Christian Life

Set a guard, O Lord, over my mouth;
Keep watch over the door of my lips.

Psalm 141:3

Keep your tongue from evil,
And your lips from speaking deceit.

Psalm 34:13

I said, "I will guard my ways,
Lest I sin with my tongue;
I will restrain my mouth with a muzzle,
While the wicked are before me."

Psalm 39:1

My tongue shall speak of Your word,
For all Your commandments are righteousness.

Psalm 119:172

And my tongue shall speak of Your righteousness
And of Your praise all the day long.

Psalm 35:28

The tongue of the wise uses knowledge rightly,
But the mouth of fools pours forth foolishness.

Proverbs 15:2

There is one who speaks like the piercings of a sword,
But the tongue of the wise promotes health.

Proverbs 12:18

When you are tempted to retaliate against your enemies

You have heard that it was said, 'An eye for an
eye and a tooth for a tooth.' But I tell you not
to resist an evil person. But whoever slaps you
on your right cheek, turn the other to him also.
If anyone wants to sue you and take away your
tunic, let him have your cloak also. And whoever
compels you to go one mile, go with him two.

Matthew 5:38-41

Beloved, let us love one another, for love is of God;
and everyone who loves is born of God and knows
God. He who does not love does not know God, for
God is love. In this the love of God was manifested
toward us, that God has sent His only begotten Son
into the world, that we might live through Him.

In this is love, not that we loved God, but that He loved us and sent His Son to be the propitiation for our sins. Beloved, if God so loved us, we also ought to love one another. No one has seen God at any time. If we love one another, God abides in us, and His love has been perfected in us.

1 John 4:7-12

You have heard that it was said, "You shall love your neighbor and hate your enemy." But I say to you, love your enemies, bless those who curse you, do good to those who hate you, and pray for those who spitefully use you and persecute you, that you may be sons of your Father in heaven; for He makes His sun rise on the evil and on the good, and sends rain on the just and on the unjust. For if you love those who love you, what reward have you? Do not even the tax collectors do the same? And if you greet your brethren only, what do you do more than others? Do not even the tax collectors do so? Therefore you shall be perfect, just as your Father in heaven is perfect.

Matthew 5:43-48

Who, when He was reviled, did not revile in
return; when He suffered, He did not threaten, but
committed Himself to Him who judges righteously.

1 Peter 2:23

Repay no one evil for evil. Have regard for good
things in the sight of all men. If it is possible, as
much as depends on you, live peaceably with all men.
Beloved, do not avenge yourselves, but rather give
place to wrath; for it is written,
"Vengeance is Mine, I will repay," says the Lord.
Therefore "If your enemy is hungry, feed him;
If he is thirsty, give him a drink;
For in so doing you will heap coals
of fire on his head."
Do not be overcome by evil, but
overcome evil with good.

Romans 12:17-21

Bless those who persecute you; bless and do not curse.

Romans 12:14

Christian Life

My enemies without cause
Hunted me down like a bird.
They silenced my life in the pit
And threw stones at me.
The waters flowed over my head;
I said, "I am cut off!"
I called on Your name, O Lord,
From the lowest pit.
You have heard my voice:
"Do not hide Your ear
From my sighing, from my cry for help."
You drew near on the day I called on You,
And said, "Do not fear!"

Lamentations 3:52-57

When gossip is a problem

Let no corrupt word proceed out of your mouth,
but what is good for necessary edification,
that it may impart grace to the hearers.

Ephesians 4:29

A perverse man sows strife,
And a whisperer separates the best of friends.

Proverbs 16:28

He who goes about as a talebearer reveals secrets;
Therefore do not associate with one who flatters
with his lips.

Proverbs 20:19

And just as you want men to do to you,
you also do to them likewise.

Luke 6:31

Where there is no wood, the fire goes out;
And where there is no talebearer, strife ceases.

Proverbs 26:20

You shall not go about as a talebearer among
your people; nor shall you take a stand against
the life of your neighbor: I am the Lord.

Leviticus 19:16

And be kind to one another, tenderhearted, forgiving
one another, even as God in Christ forgave you.

Ephesians 4:32

You shall not bear false witness
against your neighbor.

Exodus 20:16

Christian Life

If anyone among you thinks he is religious,
and does not bridle his tongue but deceives his
own heart, this one's religion is useless.

James 1:26

And whatever you do in word or deed, do
all in the name of the Lord Jesus, giving
thanks to God the Father through Him.

Colossians 3:17

When your faith is dwindling

Behold, the Lord's hand is not shortened,
That it cannot save;
Nor His ear heavy,
That it cannot hear.

Isaiah 59:1

Now faith is the substance of things hoped
for, the evidence of things not seen.

Hebrews 11:1

What then shall we say to these things? If God is for us, who can be against us? He who did not spare His own Son, but delivered Him up for us all, how shall He not with Him also freely give us all things? Who shall bring a charge against God's elect? It is God who justifies. Who is he who condemns? It is Christ who died, and furthermore is also risen, who is even at the right hand of God, who also makes intercession for us. Who shall separate us from the love of Christ? Shall tribulation, or distress, or persecution, or famine, or nakedness, or peril, or sword?

As it is written:
"For Your sake we are killed all day long;
We are accounted as sheep for the slaughter."
Yet in all these things we are more than conquerors through Him who loved us. For I am persuaded that neither death nor life, nor angels nor principalities nor powers, nor things present nor things to come, nor height nor depth, nor any other created thing, shall be able to separate us from the love of God which is in Christ Jesus our Lord.

Romans 8:31-39

Christian Life

The Lord is my light and my salvation;
Whom shall I fear?
The Lord is the strength of my life;
Of whom shall I be afraid?

Psalm 27:1

So Jesus answered and said to them, "Assuredly,
I say to you, if you have faith and do not doubt,
you will not only do what was done to the fig tree,
but also if you say to this mountain, 'Be removed
and be cast into the sea,' it will be done."

Matthew 21:21

These things I have spoken to you, that
in Me you may have peace. In the world
you will have tribulation; but be of good
cheer, I have overcome the world.

John 16:33

And He said to me, "My grace is sufficient for you,
for My strength is made perfect in weakness..."

Romans 12:9

When you are persecuted

Therefore I take pleasure in infirmities, in reproaches, in needs, in persecutions, in distresses, for Christ's sake. For when I am weak, then I am strong.

2 Corinthians 12:10

Yet if anyone suffers as a Christian, let him not be ashamed, but let him glorify God in this matter.

1 Peter 4:16

And He said to me, "My grace is sufficient for you, for My strength is made perfect in weakness..."

Romans 12:9

But the Lord is with me as a mighty, awesome One.
Therefore my persecutors will stumble,
and will not prevail.
They will be greatly ashamed,
for they will not prosper.
Their everlasting confusion will never be forgotten.

Jeremiah 20:11

Christian Life

Yes, and all who desire to live godly in
Christ Jesus will suffer persecution.

2 Timothy 3:12

If the world hates you, you know that it hated Me
before it hated you. If you were of the world, the
world would love its own. Yet because you are not of
the world, but I chose you out of the world, therefore
the world hates you. Remember the word that I said
to you, "A servant is not greater than his master."
If they persecuted Me, they will also persecute you.
If they kept My word, they will keep yours also.

John 15:18-20

Blessed are those who are persecuted
for righteousness' sake,
For theirs is the kingdom of heaven.
Blessed are you when they revile and persecute
you, and say all kinds of evil against you falsely
for My sake. Rejoice and be exceedingly glad,
for great is your reward in heaven, for so they
persecuted the prophets who were before you.

Matthew 5:10-12

And we know that all things work together
for good to those who love God, to those who
are the called according to His purpose.

Romans 8:28

For our light affliction, which is but for
a moment, is working for us a far more
exceeding and eternal weight of glory.

2 Corinthians 4:17

For consider Him who endured such hostility
from sinners against Himself, lest you become
weary and discouraged in your souls. You have not
yet resisted to bloodshed, striving against sin.

Hebrews 12:3-4

Bless those who persecute you; bless and do not curse.

Romans 12:14

It is commendable if a man bears up under
the pain of unjust suffering because he is
conscious of God. ... To this you were called,
because Christ suffered for you leaving you an
example, that you should follow in His steps.

1 Peter 2:19, 21 (NIV)

Christian Life

Yes, and all who desire to live godly in
Christ Jesus will suffer persecution.

2 Timothy 3:12

When trials overwhelm you

If you endure chastening, God deals with
you as with sons; for what son is there
whom a father does not chasten?

Hebrews 12:7

Now no chastening seems to be joyful for the
present, but painful; nevertheless, afterward
it yields the peaceable fruit of righteousness
to those who have been trained by it.

Hebrews 12:11

For what credit is it if, when you are beaten
for your faults, you take it patiently? But
when you do good and suffer, if you take it
patiently, this is commendable before God.

1 Peter 2:20

I cry out to the Lord with my voice;
With my voice to the Lord I make my supplication.
I pour out my complaint before Him;
I declare before Him my trouble.
When my spirit was overwhelmed within me,
Then You knew my path.
In the way in which I walk
They have secretly set a snare for me.
Look on my right hand and see,
For there is no one who acknowledges me;
Refuge has failed me;
No one cares for my soul.
I cried out to You, O Lord:
I said, "You are my refuge,
My portion in the land of the living.
Attend to my cry,
For I am brought very low;
Deliver me from my persecutors,
For they are stronger than I.
Bring my soul out of prison,
That I may praise Your name;
The righteous shall surround me,
For You shall deal bountifully with me."

Psalm 142

Christian Life

Happy is he who has the God of Jacob for his help
Whose hope is in the Lord his God.
Who made heaven and earth. The sea, and all
that is in them; Who keeps truth forever.

Psalm 146:5-6

Praise the Lord!
Praise the Lord, O my soul!
While I live I will praise the Lord;
I will sing praises to my God while I have my being.

Psalm 146:1-2

I will praise You with my whole heart;
Before the gods I will sing praises to You.
I will worship toward Your holy temple,
And praise Your name
For Your lovingkindness and Your truth;
For You have magnified
Your word above all Your name.
In the day when I cried out, You answered me,
And made me bold with strength in my soul.

Psalm 138:1-3

As many as I love, I rebuke and chasten.
Therefore be zealous and repent.

Revelation 3:19

Though I walk in the midst of trouble,
You will revive me;
You will stretch out Your hand
Against the wrath of my enemies,
And Your right hand will save me.
The Lord will perfect that which concerns me;
Your mercy, O Lord, endures forever;
Do not forsake the works of Your hands.

Psalm 138:7-8

There is no fear in love. But perfect love drives
out fear, because fear has to do with punishment.
The one who fears is not made perfect in love.

1 John 4:18 (NIV)

The peace of God, which transcends all
understanding, will guard your hearts
and your minds in Christ Jesus.

Philippians 4:7

Christian Life

In You, O Lord, I put my trust;
Let me never be put to shame.
Deliver me in Your righteousness,
and cause me to escape;
Incline Your ear to me, and save me.
Be my strong refuge,
To which I may resort continually;
You have given the commandment to save me,
For You are my rock and my fortress.
Deliver me, O my God,
out of the hand of the wicked,
Out of the hand of the unrighteous and cruel man.
For You are my hope, O Lord GOD;
You are my trust from my youth.
By You I have been upheld from birth;
You are He who took me out of my mother's womb.
My praise shall be continually of You.

Psalm 71:1-6

It happened after this that the people of Moab with
the people of Ammon, and others with them besides
the Ammonites, came to battle against Jehoshaphat.
Then some came and told Jehoshaphat, saying, "A
great multitude is coming against you from beyond
the sea, from Syria; and they are in Hazazon Tamar"
(which is En Gedi). And Jehoshaphat feared,
and set himself to seek the Lord, and proclaimed
a fast throughout all Judah. So Judah gathered
together to ask help from the Lord; and from all
the cities of Judah they came to seek the Lord.

Then Jehoshaphat stood in the assembly of Judah
and Jerusalem, in the house of the Lord, before the
new court, and said: "O Lord God of our fathers,
are You not God in heaven, and do You not rule over
all the kingdoms of the nations, and in Your hand is
there not power and might, so that no one is able to
withstand You? Are You not our God, who drove
out the inhabitants of this land before Your people
Israel, and gave it to the descendants of Abraham
Your friend forever? And they dwell in it, and have
built You a sanctuary in it for Your name, saying,
'If disaster comes upon us—sword, judgment,

pestilence, or famine—we will stand before this temple and in Your presence (for Your name is in this temple), and cry out to You in our affliction, and You will hear and save.' And now, here are the people of Ammon, Moab, and Mount Seir—whom You would not let Israel invade when they came out of the land of Egypt, but they turned from them and did not destroy them—here they are, rewarding us by coming to throw us out of Your possession which You have given us to inherit. O our God, will You not judge them? For we have no power against this great multitude that is coming against us; nor do we know what to do, but our eyes are upon You."

2 Chronicles 20:1-12

Not that we are sufficient of ourselves to think of anything as being from ourselves, but our sufficiency is from God, who also made us sufficient as ministers of the new covenant, not of the letter but of the Spirit, for the letter kills, but the Spirit gives life.

2 Corinthians 3:5-6

Family

When mothers need encouragement

Unto the upright there arises light in the darkness;
He is gracious, and full of compassion, and righteous.

Psalm 112:4

I will instruct you and teach you
in the way you should go;
I will guide you with My eye.

Psalm 32:8

Now to Him who is able to do exceedingly
abundantly above all that we ask or think,
according to the power that works in us...

Ephesians 3:20

The Lord is near to all who call upon Him,
To all who call upon Him in truth.

Psalm 145:18

I can do all things through Christ
who strengthens me.

Philippians 4:13

Trust in the Lord with all your heart,
And lean not on your own understanding;
In all your ways acknowledge Him,
And He shall direct your paths.

Proverbs 3:5-6

When fathers need strength

Train up a child in the way he should go,
And when he is old he will not depart from it.

Proverbs 22:6

The steps of a good man are ordered by the Lord,
And He delights in his way.
Though he fall, he shall not be utterly cast down;
For the Lord upholds him with His hand.

Psalm 37:23

As a father pities his children,
So the Lord pities those who fear Him.

Psalm 103:13

Family

Blessed are the meek,
For they shall inherit the earth.

Matthew 5:5

Hear, O Israel: The Lord our God, the Lord is one!
You shall love the Lord your God with all your
heart, with all your soul, and with all your strength.
And these words which I command you today shall
be in your heart. You shall teach them diligently to
your children, and shall talk of them when you sit
in your house, when you walk by the way, when
you lie down, and when you rise up. You shall bind
them as a sign on your hand, and they shall be as
frontlets between your eyes. You shall write them
on the doorposts of your house and on your gates.

Deuteronomy 6:4-9

But you must continue in the things which you
have learned and been assured of, knowing from
whom you have learned them, and that from
childhood you have known the Holy Scriptures,
which are able to make you wise for salvation
through faith which is in Christ Jesus.

2 Timothy 3:14-15

But those who wait on the Lord
Shall renew their strength;
They shall mount up with wings like eagles,
They shall run and not be weary,
They shall walk and not faint.

Isaiah 40:31

Blessed is that man who makes the Lord his trust,
And does not respect the proud, nor such as turn
aside to lies.

Psalm 40:4

Do not rejoice over me, my enemy;
When I fall, I will arise;
When I sit in darkness,
The Lord will be a light to me.

Micah 7:8

Have I not commanded you? Be strong and of good
courage; do not be afraid, nor be dismayed, for
the Lord your God is with you wherever you go.

Joshua 1:9

Family

Then I said to you, "Do not be terrified, or afraid
of them. The Lord your God, who goes before
you, He will fight for you, according to all He
did for you in Egypt before your eyes, and in the
wilderness where you saw how the Lord your God
carried you, as a man carries his son, in all the
way that you went until you came to this place."

Deuteronomy 1:29-31

When children need discipline

My son, do not forget my law,
But let your heart keep my commands;
For length of days and long life and
peace they will add to you.

Proverbs 3:1-2

Correct your son, and he will give you rest;
Yes, he will give delight to your soul.

Proverbs 29:17

Foolishness is bound up in the heart of a child;
The rod of correction will drive it far from him.

Proverbs 22:15

Children, obey your parents in the Lord, for this is
right. "Honor your father and mother," which is the
first commandment with promise: "that it may be
well with you and you may live long on the earth."
And you, fathers, do not provoke your
children to wrath, but bring them up in the
training and admonition of the Lord.

Ephesians 6:1-4

When husbands are at their best

Husbands, love your wives, just as Christ also
loved the church and gave Himself for her,
that He might sanctify and cleanse her with the
washing of water by the word, that He might
present her to Himself a glorious church, not
having spot or wrinkle or any such thing, but
that she should be holy and without blemish. So
husbands ought to love their own wives as their
own bodies; he who loves his wife loves himself.

Ephesians 5:25-28

Family

Husbands, likewise, dwell with them with understanding, giving honor to the wife, as to the weaker vessel, and as being heirs together of the grace of life, that your prayers may not be hindered.

1 Peter 3:7

Live joyfully with the wife whom you love all the days of your vain life which He has given you under the sun, all your days of vanity; for that is your portion in life, and in the labor which you perform under the sun.

Ecclesiastes 9:9

Let the husband render to his wife the affection due her, and likewise also the wife to her husband. The wife does not have authority over her own body, but the husband does. And likewise the husband does not have authority over his own body, but the wife does. Do not deprive one another except with consent for a time, that you may give yourselves to fasting and prayer; and come together again so that Satan does not tempt you because of your lack of self-control.

1 Corinthians 7:3-5

Yet you say, "For what reason?"
Because the Lord has been witness
Between you and the wife of your youth,
With whom you have dealt treacherously;
Yet she is your companion
And your wife by covenant.
But did He not make them one,
Having a remnant of the Spirit?
And why one?
He seeks godly offspring.
Therefore take heed to your spirit,
And let none deal treacherously
with the wife of his youth.

Malachi 2:14-15

For this reason a man shall leave his father
and mother and be joined to his wife,
and the two shall become one flesh.

Ephesians 5:31

Family

When wives are at their best

Wives, submit to your own husbands, as to the Lord.
For the husband is head of the wife, as also Christ is
head of the church; and He is the Savior of the body.
Therefore, just as the church is subject to Christ, so
let the wives be to their own husbands in everything.

Ephesians 5:22-24

Wives, likewise, be submissive to your own husbands,
that even if some do not obey the word, they, without
a word, may be won by the conduct of their wives,
when they observe your chaste conduct accompanied
by fear. Do not let your adornment be merely
outward—arranging the hair, wearing gold, or
putting on fine apparel—rather let it be the hidden
person of the heart, with the incorruptible beauty of
a gentle and quiet spirit, which is very precious in the
sight of God. For in this manner, in former times,
the holy women who trusted in God also adorned
themselves, being submissive to their own husbands.

1 Peter 3:1-5

Nevertheless let each one of you in particular
so love his own wife as himself, and let the
wife see that she respects her husband.

Ephesians 5:33

And whatever you do in word or deed, do
all in the name of the Lord Jesus, giving
thanks to God the Father through Him.

Colossians 3:17

Strength and honor are her clothing;
She shall rejoice in time to come.
She opens her mouth with wisdom,
And on her tongue is the law of kindness.
She watches over the ways of her household,
And does not eat the bread of idleness.
Her children rise up and call her blessed;
Her husband also, and he praises her:
"Many daughters have done well,
But you excel them all."
Charm is deceitful and beauty is passing,
But a woman who fears the Lord, she shall be praised.
Give her of the fruit of her hands,
And let her own works praise her in the gates.

Proverbs 31:25-31

Family

When a refresher on love is needed

Love suffers long and is kind; love does not envy;
love does not parade itself, is not puffed up; does not
behave rudely, does not seek its own, is not provoked,
thinks no evil; does not rejoice in iniquity, but rejoices
in the truth; bears all things, believes all things, hopes
all things, endures all things. Love never fails.

1 Corinthians 13:4-8a

By this we know love, because He laid down His life
for us. And we also ought to lay down our lives for
the brethren. But whoever has this world's goods, and
sees his brother in need, and shuts up his heart from
him, how does the love of God abide in him?
My little children, let us not love in word
or in tongue, but in deed and in truth.

1 John 3:16-18

Reckless words pierce like a sword, but the tongue
of the wise brings healing.

Proverbs 12:18 (NIV)

The end of a matter is better than its beginning,
and patience is better than pride. Do not be quickly
provoked in your spirit, for anger resides in the lap
of fools.

Ecclesiastes 7:8-9 (NIV)

When a marriage needs strengthening

Set me as a seal upon your heart,
As a seal upon your arm;
For love is as strong as death,
Jealousy as cruel as the grave;
Its flames are flames of fire,
A most vehement flame.
Many waters cannot quench love,
Nor can the floods drown it.
If a man would give for love
All the wealth of his house,
It would be utterly despised.

Song of Solomon 8:6-7

He who finds a wife finds a good thing,
And obtains favor form the LORD.

Proverbs 18:22

Family

Beloved, let us love one another,
for love is of God;
and everyone who loves is born of God
and knows God.
He who does not love
does not know God,
for God is love.

1 John 4:7-8

And Adam said:
"This is now bone of my bones
And flesh of my flesh;
She shall be called Woman,
Because she was taken out of Man."
Therefore a man shall leave his father and mother and
be joined to his wife, and they shall become one flesh.

Genesis 2:23-24

And may the Lord make you increase and abound
in love to one another. And to all, just as we do to
you so that He may establish your hearts blameless
in holiness before our God and Father at the coming
of our Lord Jesus Christ with all His saints.

1 Thessalonians 3:12

How fair and how pleasant you are,
O love, with your delights!
This stature of yours is like a palm tree,
And your breasts like its clusters.
I said, "I will go up to the palm tree,
I will take hold of its branches."
Let now your breasts be like clusters of the vine,
The fragrance of your breath like apples,
And the roof of your mouth like the best wine.
The wine goes down smoothly for my beloved,
Moving gently the lips of sleepers.
I am my beloved's,
And his desire is toward me.
Come, my beloved,
Let us go forth to the field;
Let us lodge in the villages.
Let us get up early to the vineyards;
Let us see if the vine has budded,
Whether the grape blossoms are open,
And the pomegranates are in bloom.
There I will give you my love.
The mandrakes give off a fragrance,
And at our gates are pleasant fruits,
All manner, new and old,
Which I have laid up for you, my beloved.

Song of Solomon 7:6-13

Family

When God is the center of the home
Through wisdom a house is built,
And by understanding it is established;
By knowledge the rooms are filled
With all precious and pleasant riches.

Proverbs 24:3-4

Blessed is the man
Who walks not in the counsel of the ungodly,
Nor stands in the path of sinners,
Nor sits in the seat of the scornful;
But his delight is in the law of the Lord,
And in His law he meditates day and night.
He shall be like a tree
Planted by the rivers of water,
That brings forth its fruit in its season,
Whose leaf also shall not wither;
And whatever he does shall prosper.

Psalm 1:1-3

If you abide in Me, and My words abide in you, you
will ask what you desire, and it shall be done for you.

John 15:7

But the end of all things is at hand; therefore be serious and watchful in your prayers. And above all things have fervent love for one another, for "love will cover a multitude of sins." Be hospitable to one another without grumbling. As each one has received a gift, minister it to one another, as good stewards of the manifold grace of God.

1 Peter 4:7-10

Unless the Lord builds the house,
They labor in vain who build it;
Unless the Lord guards the city,
The watchman stays awake in vain.

Psalm 127:1

Therefore let us pursue the things which make for peace and the things by which one may edify another.

Romans 14:19

Pleasant words are like a honeycomb,
Sweetness to the soul and health to the bones.

Proverbs 16:24

Family

Do not let any unwholesome talk come out
of your mouths, but only what is helpful for
building others up according to their needs,
that it may benefit those who listen.

Ephesians 4:29

When a critical spirit is manifested in the home

Now therefore, fear the Lord, serve Him in sincerity
and in truth, and put away the gods which your
fathers served on the other side of the River and in
Egypt. Serve the Lord! And if it seems evil to you to
serve the Lord, choose for yourselves this day whom
you will serve, whether the gods which your fathers
served that were on the other side of the River, or
the gods of the Amorites, in whose land you dwell.
But as for me and my house, we will serve the Lord.

Joshua 24:14-15

Honor your father and your mother, as the Lord
your God has commanded you, that your days
may be long, and that it may be well with you in
the land which the Lord your God is giving you.

Deuteronomy 5:16

Therefore if there is any consolation in Christ, if
any comfort of love, if any fellowship of the Spirit,
if any affection and mercy, fulfill my joy by being
like-minded, having the same love, being of one
accord, of one mind. Let nothing be done through
selfish ambition or conceit, but in lowliness of
mind let each esteem others better than himself.
Let each of you look out not only for his own
interests, but also for the interests of others.

Philippians 2:1-4

The fear of the Lord prolongs days,
But the years of the wicked will be shortened.

Proverbs 10:27

Judge not, that you be not judged. For with what
judgment you judge, you will be judged; and with
the measure you use, it will be measured back to
you. And why do you look at the speck in your
brother's eye, but do not consider the plank in your
own eye? Or how can you say to your brother, "Let
me remove the speck from your eye;" and look, a
plank is in your own eye? Hypocrite! First remove
the plank from your own eye, and then you will see
clearly to remove the speck from your brother's eye.

Matthew 7:1-5

Family

He who is of a proud heart stirs up strife,
But he who trusts in the Lord will be prospered.

Proverbs 28:25

And above all things have fervent love for one
another, for "love will cover a multitude of sins."

1 Peter 4:8

The tongue has the power of life and death.

Proverbs 18:21

When bitterness is growing

Let all bitterness, wrath, anger, clamor, and evil
speaking be put away from you, with all malice. And
be kind to one another, tenderhearted, forgiving
one another, even as God in Christ forgave you.

Ephesians 4:31-32

If we say that we have fellowship with Him, and
walk in darkness, we lie and do not practice the truth.
But if we walk in the light as He is in the light, we
have fellowship with one another, and the blood
of Jesus Christ His Son cleanses us from all sin.

1 John 1:6-7

But the fruit of the Spirit is love, joy, peace,
longsuffering, kindness, goodness, faithfulness,
gentleness, self-control. Against such there
is no law. And those who are Christ's have
crucified the flesh with its passions and desires.
If we live in the Spirit, let us also walk in the
Spirit. Let us not become conceited, provoking
one another, envying one another.

Galatians 5:22-26

He who says he is in the light, and hates his brother,
is in darkness until now. He who loves his brother
abides in the light, and there is no cause for stumbling
in him. But he who hates his brother is in darkness
and walks in darkness, and does not know where he
is going, because the darkness has blinded his eyes.

1 John 2:9-11

My little children, let us not love in word
or in tongue, but in deed and in truth.

1 John 3:18

Family

Beloved, let us love one another, for love is of God; and everyone who loves is born of God and knows God. He who does not love does not know God, for God is love. In this the love of God was manifested toward us, that God has sent His only begotten Son into the world, that we might live through Him. In this is love, not that we loved God, but that He loved us and sent His Son to be the propitiation for our sins. Beloved, if God so loved us, we also ought to love one another.

1 John 4:7-11

If someone says, "I love God," and hates his brother, he is a liar; for he who does not love his brother whom he has seen, how can he love God whom he has not seen? And this commandment we have from Him: that he who loves God must love his brother also.

1 John 4:20-21

Pursue peace with all people, and holiness, without which no one will see the Lord: looking carefully lest anyone fall short of the grace of God; lest any root of bitterness springing up cause trouble, and by this many become defiled.

Hebrews 12:14-15

When divorce is considered

For the woman who has a husband is
bound by the law to her husband as long
as he lives. But if the husband dies, she is
released from the law of her husband.

Romans 7:2

The Pharisees also came to Him, testing Him, and
saying to Him, "Is it lawful for a man to divorce his
wife for just any reason?"
And He answered and said to them, "Have you not
read that He who made them at the beginning 'made
them male and female,' and said, 'For this reason a
man shall leave his father and mother and be joined to
his wife, and the two shall become one flesh'?
So then, they are no longer two but one flesh.
Therefore what God has joined together,
let not man separate." ... And I say to you, whoever
divorces his wife, except for sexual immorality, and
marries another, commits adultery; and whoever
marries her who is divorced commits adultery."
His disciples said to Him, "If such is the case of
the man with his wife, it is better not to marry."

Matthew 19:3-6, 9-10

Family

For the Lord God of Israel says
That He hates divorce,
For it covers one's garment with violence.
Says the Lord of hosts.
Therefore take heed to your spirit,
That you do not deal treacherously.

Malachi 2:16

A man who isolates himself seeks his own desire;
He rages against all wise judgment.

Proverbs 18:1

Let your fountain be blessed,
And rejoice with the wife of your youth.
As a loving deer and a graceful doe,
Let her breasts satisfy you at all times;
And always be enraptured with her love.

Proverbs 5:18-19

Be kind and compassionate to one another, forgiving
each other, just as in Christ God forgave you.

Ephesians 4:32

Now to the married I command, yet not I but the Lord: A wife is not to depart from her husband. But even if she does depart, let her remain unmarried or be reconciled to her husband. And a husband is not to divorce his wife. But to the rest I, not the Lord, say: If any brother has a wife who does not believe, and she is willing to live with him, let him not divorce her. And a woman who has a husband who does not believe, if he is willing to live with her, let her not divorce him. For the unbelieving husband is sanctified by the wife, and the unbelieving wife is sanctified by the husband; otherwise your children would be unclean, but now they are holy. But if the unbeliever departs, let him depart; a brother or a sister is not under bondage in such cases. But God has called us to peace. For how do you know, O wife, whether you will save your husband? Or how do you know, O husband, whether you will save your wife?

1 Corinthians 7:10-16

Family

MY LITTLE CHILDREN,

LET US NOT LOVE IN WORD

OR IN TONGUE,

BUT IN DEED

AND IN TRUTH.

1 JOHN 3:18

Christian
Basics

Salvation

For all have sinned and fall short of the glory of God.

Romans 3:23

That if you confess with your mouth the Lord Jesus and believe in your heart that God has raised Him from the dead, you will be saved.

Romans 10:9

If we confess our sins, He is faithful and just to forgive us our sins and to cleanse us from all unrighteousness. If we say that we have not sinned, we make Him a liar, and His word is not in us.

1 John 1:9-10

For God so loved the world that He gave His only begotten Son, that whoever believes in Him should not perish but have everlasting life.

John 3:16

For the Son of Man has come to seek and to save that which was lost.

Luke 19:10

Most assuredly, I say to you, he who hears
My word and believes in Him who sent Me
has everlasting life, and shall not come into
judgment, but has passed from death into life.

John 5:24

The thief does not come except to steal, and to kill,
and to destroy. I have come that they may have
life, and that they may have it more abundantly.

John 10:10

Nor is there salvation in any other, for
there is no other name under heaven given
among men by which we must be saved.

Acts 4:12

For the wages of sin is death, but the gift of
God is eternal life in Christ Jesus our Lord.

Romans 6:23

For by grace you have been saved through
faith, and that not of yourselves; it is the gift of
God, not of works, lest anyone should boast.

Ephesians 2:8-9

There is therefore now no condemnation to those who are in Christ Jesus, who do not walk according to the flesh, but according to the Spirit. For the law of the Spirit of life in Christ Jesus has made me free from the law of sin and death.

Romans 8:1-2

Therefore, if anyone is in Christ, he is a new creation; old things have passed away; behold, all things have become new. Now all things are of God, who has reconciled us to Himself through Jesus Christ, and has given us the ministry of reconciliation.

2 Corinthians 5:17-18

Baptism

Therefore we were buried with Him through baptism into death, that just as Christ was raised from the dead by the glory of the Father, even so we also should walk in newness of life.

Romans 6:4

Then Peter said to them, "Repent, and let every one of you be baptized in the name of Jesus Christ for the remission of sins; and you shall receive the gift of the Holy Spirit."

Acts 2:38

And now why are you waiting? Arise and be baptized, and wash away your sins, calling on the name of the Lord.

Acts 22:16

There is also an antitype which now saves us—baptism (not the removal of the filth of the flesh, but the answer of a good conscience toward God), through the resurrection of Jesus Christ, who has gone into heaven and is at the right hand of God, angels and authorities and powers having been made subject to Him.

1 Peter 3:21-22

Buried with Him in baptism, in which you also were raised with Him through faith in the working of God, who raised Him from the dead.

Colossians 2:12

Christian Basics

Faith

For in it the righteousness of God is revealed from faith to faith; as it is written, "The just shall live by faith."

Romans 1:17

For what does the Scripture say? "Abraham believed God, and it was accounted to him for righteousness."

Romans 4:3

So then faith comes by hearing, and hearing by the word of God.

Romans 10:17

For by grace you have been saved through faith, and that not of yourselves; it is the gift of God, not of works, lest anyone should boast.

Ephesians 2:8-9

But without faith it is impossible to please Him, for he who comes to God must believe that He is, and that He is a rewarder of those who diligently seek Him.

Hebrews 11:6

My brethren, count it all joy when you
fall into various trials, knowing that the
testing of your faith produces patience.

James 1:2-3

If any of you lacks wisdom, let him ask of God, who
gives to all liberally and without reproach, and it
will be given to him. But let him ask in faith, with no
doubting, for he who doubts is like a wave of the sea
driven and tossed by the wind. For let not that man
suppose that he will receive anything from the Lord;
he is a double-minded man, unstable in all his ways.

James 1:5-8

For we walk by faith, not by sight.

2 Corinthians 5:7

When you pass through the waters, I will
be with you; and when you pass through the
rivers, they will not sweep over you. When
you walk through the fire, you will not be
burned; the flames will not set you ablaze.

Isaiah 43:2

Christian Basics

Tithing

"Bring all the tithes into the storehouse,
That there may be food in My house,
And try Me now in this,"
Says the Lord of hosts,
"If I will not open for you the windows of heaven
And pour out for you such blessing
That there will not be room enough to receive it.
"And I will rebuke the devourer for your sakes,
So that he will not destroy the fruit of your ground,
Nor shall the vine fail to bear fruit
for you in the field,"
Says the Lord of hosts;
"And all nations will call you blessed,
For you will be a delightful land,"
Says the Lord of hosts.

Malachi 3:10-12

And all the tithe of the land, whether of the
seed of the land or of the fruit of the tree,
is the Lord's. It is holy to the Lord.

Leviticus 27:30

He who is faithful in what is least is faithful also in
much; and he who is unjust in what is least is unjust
also in much. Therefore if you have not been faithful
in the unrighteous mammon, who will commit to
your trust the true riches? And if you have not been
faithful in what is another man's, who will give you
what is your own?
"No servant can serve two masters; for either
he will hate the one and love the other, or else
he will be loyal to the one and despise the other.
You cannot serve God and mammon."

Luke 16:10-13

Confession

If we confess our sins, He is faithful and
just to forgive us our sins and to cleanse
us from all unrighteousness.

John 1:9

He who covers his sins will not prosper,
But whoever confesses and forsakes
them will have mercy.

Proverbs 28:13

By this you know the Spirit of God: Every
spirit that confesses that Jesus Christ
has come in the flesh is of God.

1 John 4:2

Also I say to you, whoever confesses Me
before men, him the Son of Man also will
confess before the angels of God.

Luke 12:8

If you confess with your mouth the Lord Jesus
and believe in your heart that God has raised
Him from the dead, you will be saved.

Romans 10:9

Repentance

Now I rejoice, not that you were made sorry, but
that your sorrow led to repentance. For you were
made sorry in a godly manner, that you might suffer
loss from us in nothing. For godly sorrow produces
repentance leading to salvation, not to be regretted;
but the sorrow of the world produces death.

2 Corinthians 7:9-10

If My people who are called by My name will
humble themselves, and pray and seek My face, and
turn from their wicked ways, then I will hear from
heaven, and will forgive their sin and heal their land.

2 Chronicles 7:14

Repent therefore and be converted, that your sins
may be blotted out, so that times of refreshing
may come from the presence of the Lord.

Acts 3:19

Remember therefore from where you have
fallen; repent and do the first works, or else
I will come to you quickly and remove your
lampstand from its place—unless you repent.

Revelation 2:5

Draw near to God and He will draw near to you.
Cleanse your hands, you sinners; and purify your
hearts, you double-minded. Lament and mourn and
weep! Let your laughter be turned to mourning
and your joy to gloom. Humble yourselves in
the sight of the Lord, and He will lift you up.

James 4:8-10

He who covers his sins will not prosper,
But whoever confesses and forsakes
them will have mercy.

Proverbs 28:13

"But if a wicked man turns from all his sins which
he has committed, keeps all My statutes, and does
what is lawful and right, he shall surely live; he
shall not die. None of the transgressions which he
has committed shall be remembered against him;
because of the righteousness which he has done,
he shall live. Do I have any pleasure at all that the
wicked should die?" says the Lord God, "and not
that he should turn from his ways and live?"

Ezekiel 18:21-23

For if you thoroughly amend your ways and
your doings, if you thoroughly execute judgment
between a man and his neighbor, if you do not
oppress the stranger, the fatherless, and the
widow, and do not shed innocent blood in this
place, or walk after other gods to your hurt, then
I will cause you to dwell in this place, in the land
that I gave to your fathers forever and ever.

Jeremiah 7:5-7

Also He spoke this parable to some who trusted in themselves that they were righteous, and despised others: "Two men went up to the temple to pray, one a Pharisee and the other a tax collector. The Pharisee stood and prayed thus with himself, 'God, I thank You that I am not like other men—extortioners, unjust, adulterers, or even as this tax collector. I fast twice a week; I give tithes of all that I possess.' And the tax collector, standing afar off, would not so much as raise his eyes to heaven, but beat his breast, saying, 'God, be merciful to me a sinner!' I tell you, this man went down to his house justified rather than the other; for everyone who exalts himself will be humbled, and he who humbles himself will be exalted."

Luke 18:9-14

Then God saw their works, that they turned from their evil way; and God relented from the disaster that He had said He would bring upon them, and He did not do it.

Jonah 3:10

Repent therefore of this your wickedness,
and pray God if perhaps the thought of
your heart may be forgiven you.

Acts 8:22

Have mercy upon me, O God,
According to Your lovingkindness;
According to the multitude of Your tender mercies,
Blot out my transgressions.
Wash me thoroughly from my iniquity,
And cleanse me from my sin.
For I acknowledge my transgressions,
And my sin is always before me.
Against You, You only, have I sinned,
And done this evil in Your sight—
That You may be found just when You speak,
And blameless when You judge.
Behold, I was brought forth in iniquity,
And in sin my mother conceived me.
Behold, You desire truth in the inward parts,
And in the hidden part
You will make me to know wisdom.
Purge me with hyssop, and I shall be clean;
Wash me, and I shall be whiter than snow.

Psalm 51:1-7

And do you think this, O man, you who judge those
practicing such things, and doing the same, that
you will escape the judgment of God? Or do you
despise the riches of His goodness, forbearance,
and longsuffering, not knowing that the goodness
of God leads you to repentance? But in accordance
with your hardness and your impenitent heart you are
treasuring up for yourself wrath in the day of wrath
and revelation of the righteous judgment of God.

Romans 2:3-5

Prayer

If you abide in Me, and My words abide in you, you
will ask what you desire, and it shall be done for you.

John 15:7

Be anxious for nothing, but in everything by
prayer and supplication, with thanksgiving,
let your requests be made known to God.

Philippians 4:6

In this manner, therefore, pray:
Our Father in heaven,
Hallowed be Your name.
Your kingdom come.
Your will be done
On earth as it is in heaven.
Give us this day our daily bread.
And forgive us our debts,
As we forgive our debtors.
And do not lead us into temptation,
But deliver us from the evil one.
For Yours is the kingdom and the power
and the glory forever. Amen.

Matthew 6:9-13

I desire therefore that the men pray everywhere,
lifting up holy hands, without wrath and doubting.

1 Timothy 2:8

Now in the morning, having risen a long while
before daylight, He went out and departed
to a solitary place; and there He prayed.

Mark 1:35

So I say to you, ask, and it will be given to you; seek, and you will find; knock, and it will be opened to you. For everyone who asks receives, and he who seeks finds, and to him who knocks it will be opened. If a son asks for bread from any father among you, will he give him a stone? Or if he asks for a fish, will he give him a serpent instead of a fish? Or if he asks for an egg, will he offer him a scorpion? If you then, being evil, know how to give good gifts to your children, how much more will your heavenly Father give the Holy Spirit to those who ask Him!"

Luke 11:9-13

Rejoice always, pray without ceasing, in everything give thanks; for this is the will of God in Christ Jesus for you.

1 Thessalonians 5:16-18

Likewise the Spirit also helps in our weaknesses. For we do not know what we should pray for as we ought, but the Spirit Himself makes intercession for us with groanings which cannot be uttered.

Romans 8:26

Christian Basics

And when you pray, you shall not be like the
hypocrites. For they love to pray standing in the
synagogues and on the corners of the streets, that
they may be seen by men. Assuredly, I say to you,
they have their reward. But you, when you pray,
go into your room, and when you have shut your
door, pray to your Father who is in the secret place;
and your Father who sees in secret will reward
you openly. And when you pray, do not use vain
repetitions as the heathen do. For they think that
they will be heard for their many words. Therefore
do not be like them. For your Father knows the
things you have need of before you ask Him.

Matthew 6:5-8

If any of you lacks wisdom, let him ask of God, who
gives to all liberally and without reproach, and it will
be given to him. But let him ask in faith, with no
doubting, for he who doubts is like a wave of the sea
driven and tossed by the wind. For let not that man
suppose that he will receive anything from the Lord;
he is a double-minded man, unstable in all his ways.

James 1:5-8

Church Membership

Having been built on the foundation of the apostles
and prophets, Jesus Christ Himself being the chief
cornerstone, in whom the whole building, being
fitted together, grows into a holy temple in the
Lord, in whom you also are being built together
for a dwelling place of God in the Spirit.

Ephesians 2:20-22

So continuing daily with one accord in the
temple, and breaking bread from house to
house, they ate their food with gladness and
simplicity of heart, praising God and having
favor with all the people. And the Lord added to
the church daily those who were being saved.

Acts 2:46-47

For in fact the body is not one member but many.
If the foot should say, "Because I am not a hand, I
am not of the body," is it therefore not of the body?
And if the ear should say, "Because I am not an eye,
I am not of the body," is it therefore not of the body?
If the whole body were an eye, where would be the

hearing? If the whole were hearing, where would be the smelling? But now God has set the members, each one of them, in the body just as He pleased. And if they were all one member, where would the body be? ... That there should be no schism in the body, but that the members should have the same care for one another. And if one member suffers, all the members suffer with it; or if one member is honored, all the members rejoice with it. Now you are the body of Christ, and members individually.

1 Corinthians 12:14-19, 25-27

Now the multitude of those who believed were of one heart and one soul; neither did anyone say that any of the things he possessed was his own, but they had all things in common. And with great power the apostles gave witness to the resurrection of the Lord Jesus. And great grace was upon them all. Nor was there anyone among them who lacked; for all who were possessors of lands or houses sold them, and brought the proceeds of the things that were sold, and laid them at the apostles' feet; and they distributed to each as anyone had need.

Acts 4:32-35

These things I write to you, though I hope to come
to you shortly; but if I am delayed, I write so that
you may know how you ought to conduct yourself
in the house of God, which is the church of the
living God, the pillar and ground of the truth.

1 Timothy 3:14-15

Evangelism

And Jesus came and spoke to them, saying,
"All authority has been given to Me in heaven
and on earth. Go therefore and make disciples
of all the nations, baptizing them in the name
of the Father and of the Son and of the Holy
Spirit, teaching them to observe all things that
I have commanded you; and lo, I am with you
always, even to the end of the age." Amen.

Matthew 28:18-20

Also I heard the voice of the Lord, saying:
"Whom shall I send,
And who will go for Us?"
Then I said, "Here am I! Send me."

Isaiah 6:8

Christian Basics

But sanctify the Lord God in your hearts, and
always be ready to give a defense to everyone who
asks you a reason for the hope that is in you, with
meekness and fear; having a good conscience,
that when they defame you as evildoers, those
who revile your good conduct in Christ may be
ashamed. For it is better, if it is the will of God,
to suffer for doing good than for doing evil.

1 Peter 3:15-17

To the weak I became as weak, that I might
win the weak. I have become all things to all
men, that I might by all means save some.

1 Corinthians 9:22

The fruit of the righteous is a tree of life,
And he who wins souls is wise.

Proverbs 11:30

For Christ did not send me to baptize, but to
preach the gospel, not with wisdom of words, lest
the cross of Christ should be made of no effect.

1 Corinthians 1:17

These twelve Jesus sent out and commanded them, saying: "Do not go into the way of the Gentiles, and do not enter a city of the Samaritans. But go rather to the lost sheep of the house of Israel. And as you go, preach, saying, 'The kingdom of heaven is at hand.' Heal the sick, cleanse the lepers, raise the dead, cast out demons. Freely you have received, freely give."

Matthew 10:5-8

But God demonstrates His own love toward us, in that while we were still sinners, Christ died for us.

Romans 5:8

So then faith comes by hearing, and hearing by the word of God.

Romans 10:17

Those who are wise shall shine
Like the brightness of the firmament,
And those who turn many to righteousness
Like the stars forever and ever.

Daniel 12:3

Oh, sing to the Lord a new song!
Sing to the Lord, all the earth.
Sing to the Lord, bless His name;
Proclaim the good news of His
salvation from day to day.
Declare His glory among the nations,
His wonders among all peoples.

Psalm 96:1-3

Missions

Now the word of the Lord came to Jonah the second
time, saying, "Arise, go to Nineveh, that great city,
and preach to it the message that I tell you." So
Jonah arose and went to Nineveh, according to the
word of the Lord. Now Nineveh was an exceedingly
great city, a three-day journey in extent. And Jonah
began to enter the city on the first day's walk.
Then he cried out and said, "Yet forty days, and
Nineveh shall be overthrown!" So the people of
Nineveh believed God, proclaimed a fast, and put
on sackcloth, from the greatest to the least of them.

Jonah 3:1-5

For if I preach the gospel, I have nothing to boast of,
for necessity is laid upon me; yes, woe is me if I do
not preach the gospel! For if I do this willingly, I have
a reward; but if against my will, I have been entrusted
with a stewardship. What is my reward then? That
when I preach the gospel, I may present the gospel
of Christ without charge, that I may not abuse my
authority in the gospel.

For though I am free from all men, I have made
myself a servant to all, that I might win the more;
and to the Jews I became as a Jew, that I might win
Jews; to those who are under the law, as under the
law, that I might win those who are under the law;
to those who are without law, as without law (not
being without law toward God, but under law toward
Christ), that I might win those who are without law;
to the weak I became as weak, that I might win the
weak. I have become all things to all men, that I
might by all means save some. Now this I do for the
gospel's sake, that I may be partaker of it with you.

1 Corinthians 9:16-23

And the gospel must first be preached to all the
nations.

Mark 13:10

Christian Basics

Sing to the Lord, all the earth;
Proclaim the good news of His
salvation from day to day.
Declare His glory among the nations,
His wonders among all peoples.

1 Chronicles 16:23-24

Yet it shall not be so among you; but whoever
desires to become great among you, let him be
your servant. And whoever desires to be first
among you, let him be your slave— just as the
Son of Man did not come to be served, but to
serve, and to give His life a ransom for many.

Matthew 20:26-28

So when He had washed their feet, taken His
garments, and sat down again, He said to them,
"Do you know what I have done to you? You call
Me Teacher and Lord, and you say well, for so I
am. If I then, your Lord and Teacher, have washed
your feet, you also ought to wash one another's feet.
For I have given you an example, that you should
do as I have done to you. Most assuredly, I say to
you, a servant is not greater than his master; nor is
he who is sent greater than he who sent him. If you
know these things, blessed are you if you do them."

John 13:12-17

Armor of the Believer

Stand therefore, having girded your waist with
truth, having put on the breastplate of righteousness,
and having shod your feet with the preparation
of the gospel of peace; above all, taking the shield
of faith with which you will be able to quench all
the fiery darts of the wicked one. And take the
helmet of salvation, and the sword of the Spirit,
which is the word of God; praying always with
all prayer and supplication in the Spirit, being
watchful to this end with all perseverance and
supplication for all the saints—and for me, that
utterance may be given to me, that I may open my
mouth boldly to make known the mystery of the
gospel, for which I am an ambassador in chains;
that in it I may speak boldly, as I ought to speak.

Ephesians 6:14-20

For the word of God is living and powerful,
and sharper than any two-edged sword,
piercing even to the division of soul and spirit,
and of joints and marrow, and is a discerner
of the thoughts and intents of the heart.

Hebrews 4:12

Christian Basics

Be sober, be vigilant; because your adversary
the devil walks about like a roaring lion, seeking
whom he may devour. Resist him, steadfast in
the faith, knowing that the same sufferings are
experienced by your brotherhood in the world.

1 Peter 5:8-9

Holy Spirit

And I will pray the Father, and He will give you
another Helper, that He may abide with you forever.

John 14:16

The Spirit Himself bears witness with our
spirit that we are children of God.

Romans 8:16

Likewise the Spirit also helps in our weaknesses.
For we do not know what we should pray for as we
ought, but the Spirit Himself makes intercession
for us with groanings which cannot be uttered.

Romans 8:26

There are diversities of gifts, but the same
Spirit. There are differences of ministries, but
the same Lord. And there are diversities of
activities, but it is the same God who works
all in all. But the manifestation of the Spirit
is given to each one for the profit of all.

1 Corinthians 12:4-7

When the Day of Pentecost had fully come, they
were all with one accord in one place. And suddenly
there came a sound from heaven, as of a rushing
mighty wind, and it filled the whole house where
they were sitting. Then there appeared to them
divided tongues, as of fire, and one sat upon each of
them. And they were all filled with the Holy Spirit
and began to speak with other tongues, as the Spirit
gave them utterance…. "This Jesus God has raised
up, of which we are all witnesses. Therefore being
exalted to the right hand of God, and having received
from the Father the promise of the Holy Spirit, He
poured out this which you now see and hear."

Acts 2:1-4, 32-33

Or do you not know that your body is the temple
of the Holy Spirit who is in you, whom you have
from God, and you are not your own? For you
were bought at a price; therefore glorify God in
your body and in your spirit, which are God's.

1 Corinthians 6:19-20

And do not be drunk with wine, in which is
dissipation; but be filled with the Spirit, speaking
to one another in psalms and hymns and spiritual
songs, singing and making melody in your heart to
the Lord, giving thanks always for all things to God
the Father in the name of our Lord Jesus Christ,
submitting to one another in the fear of God.

Ephesians 5:18-21

Now the Lord is the Spirit; and where the
Spirit of the Lord is, there is liberty.

2 Corinthians 3:17

I say then: Walk in the Spirit, and you
shall not fulfill the lust of the flesh.

Galatians 5:16

In Him you also trusted, after you heard the
word of truth, the gospel of your salvation;
in whom also, having believed, you were
sealed with the Holy Spirit of promise.

Ephesians 1:13

Now hope does not disappoint, because the
love of God has been poured out in our hearts
by the Holy Spirit who was given to us.

Romans 5:5

Most assuredly, I say to you, unless one is born
of the water and the Spirit, he cannot enter the
kingdom of God. That which is born of the flesh is
flesh, and that which is born of the Spirit is spirit.

John 3:5-6

God's Will

Rejoice always, pray without ceasing,
in everything give thanks; for this is the
will of God in Christ Jesus for you.

1 Thessalonians 5:16-18

Then Jesus said to those Jews who believed Him,
"If you abide in My word, you are My disciples
indeed."

John 8:31

Trust in the Lord with all your heart,
And lean not on your own understanding;
In all your ways acknowledge Him,
And He shall direct your paths.

Proverbs 3:5-6

And do not be conformed to this world, but
be transformed by the renewing of your
mind, that you may prove what is that good
and acceptable and perfect will of God.

Romans 12:2

Come now, you who say, "Today or tomorrow we will go to such and such a city, spend a year there, buy and sell, and make a profit"; whereas you do not know what will happen tomorrow. For what is your life? It is even a vapor that appears for a little time and then vanishes away. Instead you ought to say, "If the Lord wills, we shall live and do this or that."

James 4:13-15

Therefore do not be unwise, but understand what the will of the Lord is. And do not be drunk with wine, in which is dissipation; but be filled with the Spirit, speaking to one another in psalms and hymns and spiritual songs, singing and making melody in your heart to the Lord, giving thanks always for all things to God the Father in the name of our Lord Jesus Christ, submitting to one another in the fear of God.

Ephesians 5:17-21

The Lord will perfect that which concerns me;
Your mercy, O Lord, endures forever;
Do not forsake the works of Your hands.

Psalm 138:8

Christian Basics

Therefore I exhort first of all that supplications, prayers, intercessions, and giving of thanks be made for all men, for kings and all who are in authority, that we may lead a quiet and peaceable life in all godliness and reverence. For this is good and acceptable in the sight of God our Savior, who desires all men to be saved and to come to the knowledge of the truth.

1 Timothy 2:1-4

Therefore submit yourselves to every ordinance of man for the Lord's sake, whether to the king as supreme, or to governors, as to those who are sent by him for the punishment of evildoers and for the praise of those who do good. For this is the will of God, that by doing good you may put to silence the ignorance of foolish men—as free, yet not using liberty as a cloak for vice, but as bondservants of God. Honor all people. Love the brotherhood. Fear God. Honor the king.

1 Peter 2:13-17

I delight to do Your will, O my God,
And Your law is within my heart.

Psalm 40:8

"For My thoughts are not your thoughts,
Nor are your ways My ways," says the Lord.
"For as the heavens are higher than the earth,
So are My ways higher than your ways,
And My thoughts than your thoughts."

Isaiah 55:8-9

For this is the will of God, your sanctification: that you should abstain from sexual immorality; that each of you should know how to possess his own vessel in sanctification and honor, not in passion of lust, like the Gentiles who do not know God; that no one should take advantage of and defraud his brother in this matter, because the Lord is the avenger of all such, as we also forewarned you and testified. For God did not call us to uncleanness, but in holiness.

1 Thessalonians 4:4-7

Do not repay evil with evil or insult with insult, but with blessing, because to this you were called so that you may inherit a blessing.

1 Peter 3:9

Christian Basics

Rapture

For this we say to you by the word of the Lord, that
we who are alive and remain until the coming of the
Lord will by no means precede those who are asleep.
For the Lord Himself will descend from heaven with
a shout, with the voice of an archangel, and with the
trumpet of God. And the dead in Christ will rise first.
Then we who are alive and remain shall be caught up
together with them in the clouds to meet the Lord in
the air. And thus we shall always be with the Lord.

1 Thessalonians 4:5-17

Then the sign of the Son of Man will appear in
heaven, and then all the tribes of the earth will
mourn, and they will see the Son of Man coming on
the clouds of heaven with power and great glory.
And He will send His angels with a great sound of a
trumpet, and they will gather together His elect from
the four winds, from one end of heaven to the other.

Matthew 24:30-31

And if I go and prepare a place for you, I
will come again and receive you to Myself;
that where I am, there you may be also.

John 14:3

Behold, I tell you a mystery: We shall not all
sleep, but we shall all be changed—in a moment,
in the twinkling of an eye, at the last trumpet.
For the trumpet will sound, and the dead will be
raised incorruptible, and we shall be changed.

1 Corinthians 15:51-52

For you yourselves know perfectly that the day
of the Lord so comes as a thief in the night.

1 Thessalonians 5:2

So Christ was offered once to bear the sins of many.
To those who eagerly wait for Him He will appear
a second time, apart from sin, for salvation.

Hebrews 9:28

Heaven

In My Father's house are many mansions; if it
were not so, I would have told you. I go to prepare
a place for you. And if I go and prepare a place
for you, I will come again and receive you to
Myself; that where I am, there you may be also.

John 14:2-3

And he showed me a pure river of water of life,
clear as crystal, proceeding from the throne of God
and of the Lamb. In the middle of its street, and on
either side of the river, was the tree of life, which
bore twelve fruits, each tree yielding its fruit every
month. The leaves of the tree were for the healing
of the nations. And there shall be no more curse,
but the throne of God and of the Lamb shall be in
it, and His servants shall serve Him. They shall see
His face, and His name shall be on their foreheads.
There shall be no night there: They need no lamp
nor light of the sun, for the Lord God gives them
light. And they shall reign forever and ever.

Revelation 22:1-5

But now they desire a better, that is, a heavenly country. Therefore God is not ashamed to be called their God, for He has prepared a city for them.

Hebrews 11:16

There are also celestial bodies and terrestrial bodies; but the glory of the celestial is one, and the glory of the terrestrial is another. There is one glory of the sun, another glory of the moon, and another glory of the stars; for one star differs from another star in glory.

So also is the resurrection of the dead. The body is sown in corruption, it is raised in incorruption. It is sown in dishonor, it is raised in glory. It is sown in weakness, it is raised in power. It is sown a natural body, it is raised a spiritual body. There is a natural body, and there is a spiritual body. And so it is written, "The first man Adam became a living being." The last Adam became a life-giving spirit.

1 Corinthians 15:40-45

But as it is written:
"Eye has not seen, nor ear heard,
Nor have entered into the heart of man
The things which God has prepared
for those who love Him."
But God has revealed them to us through
His Spirit. For the Spirit searches all
things, yes, the deep things of God.

1 Corinthians 2:9-10

Nevertheless we, according to His promise,
look for new heavens and a new earth
in which righteousness dwells.

2 Peter 3:13

Eternity

He has made everything beautiful in its time.
Also He has put eternity in their hearts,
except that no one can find out the work
that God does from beginning to end.

Ecclesiastes 3:11

Most assuredly, I say to you, he who hears
My word and believes in Him who sent Me
has everlasting life, and shall not come into
judgment, but has passed from death into life.

John 5:24

Blessed be the Lord God of Israel
From everlasting to everlasting!
Amen and Amen.

Psalm 41:13

Before the mountains were brought forth,
Or ever You had formed the earth and the world,
Even from everlasting to everlasting, You are God.

Psalm 90:2

Then Jesus said to them, "Most assuredly, I say to you, unless you eat the flesh of the Son of Man and drink His blood, you have no life in you. Whoever eats My flesh and drinks My blood has eternal life, and I will raise him up at the last day. For My flesh is food indeed, and My blood is drink indeed. He who eats My flesh and drinks My blood abides in Me, and I in him. As the living Father sent Me, and I live because of the Father, so he who feeds on Me will live because of Me. This is the bread which came down from heaven—not as your fathers ate the manna, and are dead. He who eats this bread will live forever."

John 6:53-58

Spiritual Growth

Be diligent to present yourself approved to God, a worker who does not need to be ashamed, rightly dividing the word of truth.

2 Timothy 2:15

Blessed are those who hunger and thirst for righteousness, for they shall be filled.

Matthew 5:6

But also for this very reason, giving all diligence,
add to your faith virtue, to virtue knowledge,
to knowledge self-control, to self-control
perseverance, to perseverance godliness, to
godliness brotherly kindness, and to brotherly
kindness love. For if these things are yours and
abound, you will be neither barren nor unfruitful
in the knowledge of our Lord Jesus Christ.

2 Peter 1:5-8

Nevertheless we, according to His promise,
look for new heavens and a new earth in which
righteousness dwells. Therefore, beloved, looking
forward to these things, be diligent to be found
by Him in peace, without spot and blameless.

2 Peter 3:13-14

Therefore bear fruits worthy of repentance, and do
not think to say to yourselves, "We have Abraham
as our father." For I say to you that God is able to
raise up children to Abraham from these stones.
And even now the ax is laid to the root of the
trees. Therefore every tree which does not bear
good fruit is cut down and thrown into the fire.

Matthew 3:8-10

Christian Basics

You did not choose Me, but I chose you and
appointed you that you should go and bear fruit,
and that your fruit should remain, that whatever
you ask the Father in My name He may give you.

John 15:16

And He Himself gave some to be apostles, some
prophets, some evangelists, and some pastors and
teachers, for the equipping of the saints for the
work of ministry, for the edifying of the body of
Christ, till we all come to the unity of the faith and
of the knowledge of the Son of God, to a perfect
man, to the measure of the stature of the fullness
of Christ; that we should no longer be children,
tossed to and fro and carried about with every wind
of doctrine, by the trickery of men, in the cunning
craftiness of deceitful plotting, but, speaking the
truth in love, may grow up in all things into Him
who is the head—Christ— from whom the whole
body, joined and knit together by what every joint
supplies, according to the effective working by
which every part does its share, causes growth
of the body for the edifying of itself in love.

Ephesians 4:11-16

All Scripture is given by inspiration of God,
and is profitable for doctrine, for reproof, for
correction, for instruction in righteousness,

2 Timothy 3:16

My brethren, count it all joy when you fall
into various trials, knowing that the testing
of your faith produces patience. But let
patience have its perfect work, that you may
be perfect and complete, lacking nothing.

James 1:2-4

Blessed is the man
Who walks not in the counsel of the ungodly,
   Nor stands in the path of sinners,
   Nor sits in the seat of the scornful;
But his delight is in the law of the Lord,
   And in His law he meditates day and night.
He shall be like a tree
   Planted by the rivers of water,
   That brings forth its fruit in its season,
   Whose leaf also shall not wither;
And whatever he does shall prosper.

Psalm 1:1-3

Christian Basics

My son, keep my words,
And treasure my commands and live,
And my law as the apple of your eye.
Bind them on your fingers;
Write them on the
tablet of your heart.

Proverbs 7:1-3

Pursue peace with all people, and holiness,
without which no one will see the Lord; looking
carefully lest anyone fall short of the grace of
God; lest any root of bitterness springing up cause
trouble, and by this many become defiled.

Hebrews 12:14-15

Resources *from* Dr. David Jeremiah

When Your World Falls Apart

Have you ever wondered…why this? Why me? Why now? In this perceptive and deeply personal book, pastor and teacher David Jeremiah draws from the beautiful poetry and deep truths of the Psalms to gain strength on his journey into the unknown of serious illness. Interwoven with his own reflections and insights are the inspiring real-life stories of other men and women who have faced unexpected adversity—and found that God's grace truly is sufficient for every need.

Available in book, study guide, and audio CD.

In the Words of David Jeremiah

Some days we need a word, a thought, to encourage us and keep us moving toward the goal of being a light for God. In this collection of quotations from David Jeremiah, you will find nuggets of truth to ponder and keep close to your heart. This book contains more than 300 quotes taken from published works of David Jeremiah on topics such as: faith, trials, purpose, hope, encouragement, and contentment, topically divided into three sections: Your Personal Faith, Your Christian Walk, Your Future Hope. This book is a great resource for personal study or to share with a friend.

The Unchanging Word of God

Since the inception of the Turning Point for
God ministry in 1982, one thing has remained a
constant—the commitment to the Word of God.
During the past thirty years, Dr. David Jeremiah
has devoted this ministry to teaching about
The Unchanging Word of God wherever and
whenever he has been given the opportunity.
Dr. Jeremiah has selected twenty chapters from
selected books he has written during his ministry
and they are compiled in this unique book—
serving as a poignant reminder that the truth
of God's Word is unchanging.

For more...

For more information about Turning
Point resources, visit our website at
www.DavidJeremiah.org.

WHERE TO GO IN THE BIBLE WHEN...

SCRIPTURE
REFERENCE
GUIDE

88 TOPICS

DR. DAVID JEREMIAH